TOLD UNDER CANVAS
BUG-JARGAL

by

VICTOR HUGO

Copyright © 2016 Read Books Ltd.
This book is copyright and may not be
reproduced or copied in any way without
the express permission of the publisher in writing

British Library Cataloguing-in-Publication Data
A catalogue record for this book is available from
the British Library

CONTENTS

Victor Hugo	5
PROLOGUE	11
CHAPTER I.	20
CHAPTER II.	24
CHAPTER III.	26
CHAPTER IV.	29
CHAPTER V.	32
CHAPTER VI.	36
CHAPTER VII.	38
CHAPTER VIII.	41
CHAPTER IX.	43
CHAPTER X.	47
CHAPTER XI.	49
CHAPTER XII.	52
CHAPTER XIII.	54
CHAPTER XIV.	62
CHAPTER XV.	64
CHAPTER XVI.	66
CHAPTER XVII.	68
CHAPTER XVIII.	70
CHAPTER XIX.	72
CHAPTER XX.	74
CHAPTER XXI.	77
CHAPTER XXII.	79
CHAPTER XXIII.	81
CHAPTER XXIV.	85
CHAPTER XXV.	87
CHAPTER XXVI.	93
CHAPTER XXVII.	97

CHAPTER XXVIII	98
CHAPTER XXIX	109
CHAPTER XXX	111
CHAPTER XXXI	119
CHAPTER XXXII	123
CHAPTER XXXIII	128
CHAPTER XXXIV	131
CHAPTER XXXV	132
CHAPTER XXXVI	137
CHAPTER XXXVII	138
CHAPTER XXXVIII	142
CHAPTER XXXIX	145
CHAPTER XL	150
CHAPTER XLI	153
CHAPTER XLII	156
CHAPTER XLIII	160
CHAPTER XLIV	163
CHAPTER XLV	165
CHAPTER XLVI	168
CHAPTER XLVII	170
CHAPTER XLVIII	174
CHAPTER XLIX	176
CHAPTER L	182
CHAPTER LI	185
CHAPTER LII	191
CHAPTER LIII	192
CHAPTER LIV	193
CHAPTER LV	195
EPILOGUE	199

Victor Hugo

Victor Marie Hugo was born on 26th February 1802, in Besançon, Franche-Comté, France. He was a political campaigner, artist, poet, novelist and dramatist of the Romantic movement, considered one of the greatest French writers of all time.

Hugo's father was a freethinking republican who considered Napoléon a hero, and his mother was a Catholic Royalist, who was executed in 1812 for plotting against the legendary general. Hugo's childhood was a period of national political turmoil. Napoléon was proclaimed Emperor two years after Hugo's birth, and the Bourbon Monarchy was restored before his eighteenth birthday. The opposing political and religious views of Hugo's parents reflected the forces that would battle for supremacy in France throughout his life.

As a young man, his mother dominated his education and upbringing, and as a result Hugo's early work in poetry and fiction reflects her passionate devotion to both King and Faith. It was only later, during the events leading up to France's 1848 Revolution, that he would begin to rebel against his Catholic Royalist education and instead champion Republicanism and Freethought. Hugo was also a rebellious young man, and on falling in love with his childhood friend Adèle Foucher (1803–

1868), became secretly engaged against his mothers wishes. Because of his close relationship with his mother, Hugo waited until after his mother's death (in 1821) to marry Adèle in 1822.

Hugo published his first novel the year following his marriage (*Han d'Islande*, 1823), and his second three years later (*Bug-Jargal*, 1826). Between 1829 and 1840 he would publish five more volumes of poetry, cementing his reputation as one of the greatest elegiac and lyric poets of his time. Victor Hugo's first mature work of fiction appeared in 1829, and reflected the acute social conscience that would infuse his later work. *The Last Day of a Condemned Man* would have a profound influence on later writers such as Albert Camus, Charles Dickens, and Fyodor Dostoevsky. It was soon followed by *The Hunchback of Notre-Dame* (in 1831), which was quickly translated into other language across Europe.

Adèle and Victor Hugo had their first child, Léopold, in 1823, but the boy died in infancy. The following year, on 28th August 1824, the couple's second child, Léopoldine was born, followed by Charles in 1826, François-Victor in 1828, and Adèle in 1830. Hugo's oldest and favourite daughter, Léopoldine, died at the age of nineteen in 1843, shortly after her marriage to Charles Vacquerie. On 4th September 1843, she drowned in the Seine at Villequier, pulled down by her heavy skirts, when a boat overturned. Her young husband also died trying to save her. The death left her father devastated; Hugo was travelling with his mistress at the time in the south of France, and first learned about Léopoldine's death from a newspaper he read in a cafe.

Hugo wrote many poems about his daughter's tragic life and death, and many biographers have claimed that he never completely recovered from this traumatic incident. His most famous poem is probably *Demain, Dès L'aube*, in which he describes visiting her grave. He began planning a major novel about social misery and injustice as early as the 1830s, but it would take a full seventeen years for *Les Misérables* to be realized and finally published in 1862. On its publication, the critical establishment was generally hostile to the novel, with Gustave Flaubert claiming he found within it 'neither truth nor greatness' and Baudelaire castigating it as 'tasteless and inept.' Despite this, *Les Misérables* was a massive hit with the public, and today remains Victor Hugo's most enduringly popular work.

After three unsuccessful attempts, Hugo was finally elected to the Académie Française in 1841, solidifying his position in the world of French arts and letters. He was also elevated to the peerage by King Louis-Philippe in the same year and entered the Higher Chamber as a *pair de France*, where he spoke against the death penalty and social injustice, and in favour of freedom of the press and self-government for Poland. In 1848, Hugo was elected to the Parliament as a conservative. In 1849 he broke with the conservatives when he gave a noted speech calling for the end of misery and poverty. When Louis Napoleon (Napoleon III) seized complete power in 1851, establishing an anti-parliamentary constitution, Hugo openly declared him a traitor to France.

Hugo decided to live in exile after Napoleon III's coup d'état at the end of 1851. After leaving France, he lived in Brussels briefly in 1851, before moving to the Channel Islands, first to Jersey (1852–1855) and then to the smaller island of Guernsey in 1855, where he stayed until 1870. Whilst in exile, Hugo published his famous political pamphlets against Napoleon

III, *Napoléon le Petit* and *Histoire d'un Crime,* which whilst banned in France, had a strong impact. Although Napoleon III proclaimed a general amnesty in 1859, the author stayed in exile, only returning when Napoleon was forced from power in 1870. Hugo's next novel, *Troilers of the Sea* turned away from the social and political themes so prevalent in Les Miserables. It told the story of a man hoping to gain the approval of his beloved's father by rescuing his ship - thus battling the elements, mythical beasts and the sea itself. It was published in 1866, and was dedicated to the channel islands, in which Hugo found such a welcoming home.

Hugo returned to political and social issues in his next novel, *The Man Who Laughs*, which was published in 1869 and painted a critical picture of the aristocracy. The novel was not as successful as his previous efforts, and Hugo himself began to comment on the growing distance between himself and literary contemporaries such as Flaubert and Émile Zola, whose realist and naturalist novels were now exceeding the popularity of his own work. After the Siege of Paris, Hugo lived again in Guernsey from 1872 to 1873, before finally returning to France for the remainder of his life. His last novel, *Ninety-Three*, published in 1874, dealt with a subject that Hugo had previously avoided: the Reign of Terror during the French Revolution. Though Hugo's popularity was on the decline at the time of its publication, many now consider *Ninety-Three* to be a work on par with his earlier and better-known novels.

When Hugo returned to Paris in 1870, the country hailed him as a national hero. This was a sad time for the ageing writer however, as within a brief period he suffered a mild stoke, his daughter Adèle's internment in an insane asylum, and the death of his two sons. His wife Adèle had died in 1868. Hugo's mistress, Juliette Drouet, also died in 1883 – two years before Hugo's own death. Despite this, to honour the fact that he was entering his eightieth year, in 1882, one of the greatest tributes to a living writer was held. The celebrations began on 25th June when Hugo was presented with a Sèvres vase, the traditional gift for sovereigns, and on 27th June one of the largest parades in French history was held.

Victor Hugo's death from pneumonia on 22nd May 1885, at the age of eighty-three, generated intense national mourning. He was not only revered as a towering figure in literature, but he was also a statesman who shaped the Third Republic and democracy in France. More than two million people joined his funeral procession in Paris from the Arc de Triomphe to the Panthéon, where he was buried. He shares a crypt within the with Alexandre Dumas and Émile Zola.

TOLD UNDER CANVAS
BUG-JARGAL

PROLOGUE

When it came to the turn of Captain Leopold d'Auverney, he gazed around him with surprise, and hurriedly assured his comrades that he did not remember any incident in his life that was worthy of repetition.

"But, Captain d'Auverney," objected Lieutenant Henri, "you have—at least report says so—travelled much, and seen a good deal of the world; have you not been to the Antilles, to Africa, and to Italy? and above all, you have been in Spain——But see, here is your lame dog come back again!"

D'Auverney started, let fall the cigar that he was smoking, and turned quickly to the tent door, at which an enormous dog appeared, limping towards him.

In another instant the dog was licking his feet, wagging his tail, whining, and gamboling as well as he was able; and by every means testifying his delight at finding his master. And at last, as if he felt that he had done all that could be required of a dog, he curled himself up peaceably before his master's seat.

Captain d'Auverney was much moved, but he strove to conceal his feelings, and mechanically caressed the dog with one hand, whilst with the other he played with the chin-strap of his shako, murmuring from time to time, "So here you are once again, Rask, here you are." Then, as if suddenly recollecting himself, he exclaimed aloud, "But who has brought him back?"

"By your leave, captain——"

For the last few seconds Sergeant Thaddeus had been standing at the door of the tent, the curtain of which he was holding back with his left hand, whilst his right was thrust into the bosom of his great-coat. Tears were in his eyes as he contemplated the meeting of the dog and his master, and at last, unable to keep silence any longer, he risked the words—

"By your leave, captain——"

D'Auverney raised his eyes.

"Why, it is you, Thaddeus; and how the deuce have you been able—eh? Poor dog, poor Rask, I thought that you were in the English camp. Where did you find him, sergeant?"

"Thanks be to heaven, captain, you see me as happy as your little nephew used to be when you let him off his Latin lesson."

"But tell me, where *did* you find him?"

"I did not find him, captain; I went to look for him."

Captain d'Auverney rose, and offered his hand to the sergeant, but the latter still kept his in the bosom of his coat.

"Well, you see, it was—at least, captain, since poor Rask was lost, I noticed that you were like a man beside himself; so when I saw that he did not come to me in the evening, according to his custom, for his share of my ration bread—which made old

Thaddeus weep like a child, I, who before that had only wept twice in my life, the first time when—yes, the day when——" and the sergeant cast a sad look upon his captain. "Well, the second was when that scamp Balthazar, the corporal of the 7th half brigade, persuaded me to peel a bunch of onions."

"It seems to me, Thaddeus," cried Henri, with a laugh, "that you avoid telling us what was the first occasion upon which you shed tears."

"It was doubtless, old comrade," said the captain kindly, as he patted Rask's head, "when you answered the roll-call as Tour d'Auvergne, the first grenadier of France."

"No, no, captain; if Sergeant Thaddeus wept, it was when he gave the order to fire on Bug-Jargal, otherwise called Pierrot."

A cloud gathered on the countenance of D'Auverney, then he again endeavoured to clasp the sergeant's hand; but in spite of the honour that was attempted to be conferred on him, the old man still kept his hand hidden under his coat.

"Yes, captain," continued Thaddeus, drawing back a step or two, whilst D'Auverney fixed his eyes upon him with a strange and sorrowful expression. "Yes, I wept for him that day, and he well deserved it. He was black, it is true, but gunpowder is black also, and—and——"

The good sergeant would fain have followed out his strange comparison, for there was evidently something in the idea that pleased him; but he utterly failed to put his thoughts into words, and after having attacked his idea on every side, as a general would a fortified place, and failed, he raised the siege, and without noticing the smiles of his officers, he continued:

"Tell me, captain, do you recollect how that poor negro arrived all out of breath, at the moment that his ten comrades were waiting on the spot?—we had had to tie them though. It was I who commanded the party; and when with his own hands he untied them, and took their place, although they did all that they could to dissuade him; but he was inflexible. Ah, what a man he was; you might as well have tried to move Gibraltar! And then, captain, he drew himself up as if he were going to enter a ballroom, and this dog, who knew well enough what was coming, flew at my throat——"

"Generally, Thaddeus, at this point of your story, you pat Rask," interrupted the captain; "see how he looks at you."

"You are right, sir," replied Thaddeus, with an air of embarrassment; "he *does* look at me, poor fellow—but the old woman Malajuda told me it was unlucky to pat a dog with the left hand, and——"

"And why not with your right, pray?" asked D'Auverney, for the first time noticing the sergeant's pallor, and the hand reposing in his bosom.

The sergeant's discomfort appeared to increase.

"By your leave, captain, it is because—well, you have got a lame dog, and now there is a chance of your having a one-handed sergeant."

"A one-handed sergeant! What do you mean? Let me see your arm. One hand! Great heavens!"

D'Auverney trembled, as the sergeant slowly withdrew his hand from his bosom, and showed it enveloped in a blood-stained handkerchief.

"This is terrible," exclaimed D'Auverney, carefully undoing the bandage. "But tell me, old comrade, how this happened."

"As for that, the thing is simple enough. I told you how I had noticed your grief since those confounded English had taken away your dog, poor Rask, Bug's dog. I made up my mind to-day to bring him back, even if it cost me my life, so that you might eat a good supper. After having told Mathelet, your *bât* man, to get out and brush your full-dress uniform, as we are to go into action to-morrow, I crept quietly out of camp, armed only with my sabre, and crouched under the hedges until I neared the English camp. I had not passed the first trench, when I saw a whole crowd of red soldiers. I crept on quietly to see what they were doing, and in the midst of them I perceived Rask tied to a tree; whilst two of the *milords*, stripped to here, were knocking each other about with their fists, until their bones sounded like the big drum of the regiment. They were fighting for your dog. But when Rask caught sight of me, he gave such a bound, that the rope broke, and in the twinkling of an eye the rogue was after me. I did not stop to explain, but off I ran, with all the English at my heels. A regular hail of balls whistled past my ears. Rask barked, but they could not hear him for their shouts of 'French dog! French dog!' just as if Rask was not of the pure St. Domingo breed. In spite of all I crushed through the thicket, and had almost got clean away, when two red coats confronted me. My sabre accounted for one, and would have rid me of the other, had his pistol not unluckily had a bullet in it. My right arm suffered; but 'French dog' leapt at his throat, as if he were an old acquaintance. Down fell the Englishman, for the embrace was so tight that he was strangled in a moment—and here we both are. My only regret is that I did not get my wound in to-morrow's battle."

"Thaddeus, Thaddeus!" exclaimed the captain in tones of reproach; "were you mad enough to expose your life thus for a dog?"

"It was not for a dog, it was for Rask."

D'Auverney's face softened as Thaddeus added—"For Rask, for Bug's dog."

"Enough, enough, old comrade!" cried the captain, dashing his hand across his eyes; "come, lean on me, and I will lead you to the hospital."

Thaddeus essayed to decline the honour, but in vain; and as they left the tent the dog got up and followed them.

This little drama had excited the curiosity of the spectators to the highest degree. Captain Leopold d'Auverney was one of those men who, in whatever position the chances of nature and society may place them, always inspire a mingled feeling of interest and respect. At the first glimpse there was nothing striking in him—his manner was reserved, and his look cold. The tropical sun, though it had browned his cheek, had not imparted to him that vivacity of speech and gesture which amongst the Creoles is united to an easy carelessness of demeanour, in itself full of charm.

D'Auverney spoke little, listened less, but showed himself ready to act at any moment. Always the first in the saddle, and the last to return to camp, he seemed to seek a refuge from his thoughts in bodily fatigue. These thoughts, which had marked his brow with many a premature wrinkle, were not of the kind that you can get rid of by confiding them to a friend; nor could they be discussed in idle conversation. Leopold d'Auverney, whose body the hardships of war could not subdue, seemed to experience a sense of insurmountable fatigue in what is termed the conflict of the feelings. He avoided argument as much as he sought warfare. If at any time he allowed himself to be drawn into a discussion, he would utter a few words full of common sense and reason, and then at the moment of triumph over his antagonist he would stop short, and muttering "What good is it?" would saunter off to the commanding officer to glean what information he could regarding the enemy's movements.

His comrades forgave his cold, reserved, and silent habits, because upon every occasion they had found him kind, gentle, and benevolent. He had saved many a life at the risk of his own, and they well knew that though his mouth was rarely opened, yet his purse was never closed when a comrade had need of his assistance.

He was young; many would have guessed him at thirty years of age, but they would have been wrong, for he was some years under it. Although he had for a long period fought in the ranks of the Republican army, yet all were in ignorance of his former life. The only one to whom he seemed ever to open his heart was Sergeant Thaddeus, who had joined the regiment with him, and would at times speak vaguely of sad events in his early life. It was known that D'Auverney had undergone great misfortunes in America, that he had been married in St. Domingo, and that his wife and all his family had perished in those terrible massacres which had marked the Republican invasion of that magnificent colony. At the time of which we write, misfortunes of this kind were so general, that any one could sympathize with, and feel pity for, such sufferers.

D'Auverney, therefore, was pitied less for his misfortunes than for the manner in which they had been brought about.

Beneath his icy mask of indifference the traces of the incurably wounded spirit could be at times perceived.

When he went into action his calmness returned, and in

the fight he behaved as if he sought for the rank of general; whilst after victory he was as gentle and unassuming as if the position of a private soldier would have satisfied his ambition. His comrades, seeing him thus despise honour and promotion, could not understand what it was that lighted up his countenance with a ray of hope when the action commenced, and they did not for a moment divine that the prize D'Auverney was striving to gain was simply—*Death*.

The Representatives of the People, in one of their missions to the army, had appointed him a Chief of Brigade on the field of battle; but he had declined the honour upon learning that it would remove him from his old comrade Sergeant Thaddeus.

Some days afterwards, having returned from a dangerous expedition safe and sound, contrary to the general expectation and his own hopes, he was heard to regret the rank that he had refused.

"For," said he, "since the enemy's guns always spare me, perhaps the guillotine, which ever strikes down those it has raised, would in time have claimed me."

Such was the character of the man upon whom the conversation turned as soon as he had left the tent.

"I would wager," cried Lieutenant Henri, wiping a splash of mud off his boot which the dog had left as he passed him, "I would wager that the captain would not exchange the broken paw of his dog for the ten baskets of Madeira that we caught a glimpse of in the general's waggon."

"Bah!" cried Paschal, the aide-de-camp, "that would be a bad bargain: the baskets are empty by now, and thirty empty bottles would be a poor price for a dog's paw—why, you might make a good bell-handle out of it."

They all laughed at the grave manner in which Paschal pronounced these words, with the exception of a young officer of Hussars named Alfred, who remarked—

"I do not see any subject for chaff in this matter, gentlemen. This sergeant and dog, who are always at D'Auverney's heels ever since I have known him, seem to me more the objects of sympathy than raillery, and interest me greatly."

Paschal, annoyed that his wit had missed fire, interrupted him. "It certainly is a most sentimental scene—a lost dog found, and a broken arm——"

"Captain Paschal," said Henri, throwing an empty bottle outside the tent, "you are wrong; this Bug, otherwise called Pierrot, excites my curiosity greatly."

At this moment D'Auverney returned, and sat down without uttering a word. His manner was still sad, but his face was more calm; he seemed not to have heard what was said. Rask, who had followed him, lay down at his feet, but kept a watchful eye on his master's comrades.

"Pass your glass, Captain d'Auverney, and taste this."

"Oh, thank you," replied the captain, evidently imagining that he was answering a question, "the wound is not dangerous—there is no bone broken."

The respect which all felt for D'Auverney prevented a burst of laughter at this reply.

"Since your mind is at rest regarding Thaddeus' wound," said Henri, "and, as you may remember, we entered into an agreement to pass away the hours of bivouac by relating to each other our adventures, will you carry out your promise by telling us the history of your lame dog, and of Bug—otherwise called Pierrot, that regular Gibraltar of a man?"

To this request, which was put in a semi-jocular tone, D'Auverney at last yielded.

"I will do what you ask, gentlemen," said he; "but you must only expect a very simple tale, in which I play an extremely second rate part. If the affection that exists between Thaddeus, Rask, and myself leads you to expect anything very wonderful, I fear that you will be greatly disappointed. However, I will begin."

For a moment D'Auverney relapsed into thought, as though he wished to recall past events which had long since been replaced in his memory by the acts of his later years; but at last, in a low voice and with frequent pauses, he began his tale.

CHAPTER I.

"I was born in France, but at an early age I was sent to St. Domingo, to the care of an uncle to whose daughter it had been arranged between our parents that I was to be married. My uncle was one of the wealthiest colonists, and possessed a magnificent house and extensive plantations in the Plains of Acul, near Fort Galifet.

"The position of the estate, which no doubt you wonder at my describing so minutely, was one of the causes of all our disasters, and the eventual total ruin of our whole family.

"Eight hundred negro slaves cultivated the enormous domains of my uncle. Sad as the position of a slave is, my uncle's hardness of heart added much to the unhappiness of those who had the misfortune to be his property.

"My uncle was one of the happily small number of planters from whom despotic power had taken away the gentler feelings of humanity. He was accustomed to see his most trifling command unhesitatingly obeyed, and the slightest delay on the part of his slaves in carrying it out was punished with the harshest severity; whilst the intercession either of my cousin or of myself too often merely led to an increase of the punishment, and we were only too often obliged to rest satisfied by secretly assuaging the injuries which we were powerless to prevent.

"Amongst the multitude of his slaves, one only had found favour in my uncle's sight; this was a half-caste Spanish dwarf, who had been given him by Lord Effingham, the Governor of Jamaica.

"My uncle, who had for many years resided in Brazil, and had adopted the luxurious habits of the Portuguese, loved to surround himself with an establishment that was in keeping with his wealth. In order that nothing should be wanting, he had made the slave presented to him by Lord Effingham his fool, in imitation of the feudal lords who had jesters attached to their households. I must say that the slave amply fulfilled all the required conditions. Habibrah, for that was the half-caste's name, was one of those strangely-formed, or, rather, deformed beings, who would be looked upon as monsters if their very hideousness did not cause a laugh. This ill-featured dwarf was short and fat, and moved with wondrous activity upon a pair of slender limbs, which, when he sat down, bent under him like the legs of a spider. His enormous head, covered with a mass of red curly wool, was stuck between his shoulders, whilst his ears were so large that Habibrah's comrades were in the habit of saying that he used them to wipe his eyes when he wept. On his face there was always a grin, which was continually changing its character, and which caused his ugliness to be of an ever-varying description. My uncle was fond of him, because of his extreme hideousness and his inextinguishable gaiety. Habibrah was his only favourite, and led a life of ease, whilst the other slaves were overwhelmed with work. The sole duties of the jester were to carry a large fan, made of the feathers of the bird of paradise, to keep away the sandflies and the mosquitoes from his master. At meal-times he sat upon a reed mat at his master's feet, who fed him with tit-bits from his own plate. Habibrah appeared to appreciate all these acts of kindness, and at the slightest sign from my uncle he would run to him with the agility of a monkey and the docility of a dog.

"I had imbibed a prejudice against my uncle's favourite slave. There was something crawling in his servility, and though outdoor slavery does not dishonour, domestic service too often debases. I felt a sentiment of pity for those slaves who toiled in the scorching sun, with scarcely a vestige of clothing to hide their chains; but I despised this idle serf, with his garments ornamented with gold lace and adorned with bells. Besides, the dwarf never made use of his influence with his master to ameliorate the condition of his fellow-sufferers; on the contrary, I heard him once, when he thought that he and his master were alone, urge him to increase his severity towards his ill-fated comrades.

"The other slaves, however, did not appear to look upon him with any feelings of anger or rancour, but treated him with a timid kind of respect; and when, dressed in all the splendour of laced garments, and a tall pointed cap ornamented with bells and quaint symbols traced upon it in red ink, he walked past their huts, I have heard them murmur in accents of awe, "He is an *obi*" (sorcerer).

"These details, to which I now draw your attention, occupied my mind but little then. I had given myself up entirely to the emotion of a pure love in which nothing else could mingle; a love which was returned me with passion by the girl to whom I was betrothed, and I gave little heed to anything that was not Marie!

"Accustomed from youth to look upon her as the future companion of my life, there was a curious mixture of the love of a brother for a sister, mingled with the passionate adoration of a betrothed lover.

"Few men have spent their earlier years more happily than I have done, or have felt their souls expand into life in the midst of a delicious climate and all the luxuries which wealth could procure, with perfect happiness in the present and the brightest hopes for the future. No man, as I said before, could have spent their earlier years more happily——"

D'Auverney paused for a moment, as if these thoughts of bygone happiness had stilled his voice, and then added—

"And no one could have passed his later ones in more profound misery and affliction."

CHAPTER II.

In the midst of these blind illusions and hopes, my twentieth birthday approached. It was now the month of August, 1791, and my uncle had decided that this should be the date of my marriage with Marie. You can well understand that the thoughts of happiness, now so near, absorbed all my faculties, and how little notice I took of the political crisis which was then felt throughout the colony. I will not, therefore, speak of the Count de Pernier, or of M. de Blanchelande, nor of the tragical death of the unfortunate Colonel de Marchiste; nor will I attempt to describe the jealousies of the Provincial House of Assembly of the North, and the Colonial Assembly, which afterwards called itself the General Assembly, declaring that the word "Colonial" had a ring of slavery in it.

For my own part, I sided with neither; and if I did espouse any cause, it was in favour of Cap, near which town my home was situate, in opposition to Port au Prince.

Only once did I mix myself up in the question of the day. It was on the occasion of the disastrous decree of the 15th of May, 1791, by which the National Assembly of France admitted free men of colour to enjoy the same political privileges as the whites.

At a ball given by the Governor of Cap, many of the younger colonists spoke in impassioned terms of this law, which levelled so cruel a blow at the instincts of supremacy assumed by the whites, with perhaps too little foundation. I had, as yet, taken no part in the conversation, when I saw approaching the group a wealthy planter, whose doubtful descent caused him to be received merely upon sufferance by the white society. I stepped in front of him, and in a haughty voice I exclaimed, "Pass on, sir! pass on! or you may hear words which would certainly be disagreeable to those with *mixed blood* in their veins."

He was so enraged at this insinuation, that he challenged me. We fought, and each was slightly wounded. I confess that I was in the wrong to have thus provoked him, and it is probable that I should not have done so on a mere *question of colour,* but I had for some time past noticed that he had had the audacity to pay certain attentions to my cousin, and had danced with her the very night upon which I had insulted him.

However, as time went on, and the date so ardently desired approached, I was a perfect stranger to the state of political ferment in which those around me lived; and I never perceived the frightful cloud which already almost obscured the horizon, and which promised a storm that would sweep all before it.

No one at that time thought seriously of a revolt amongst the slaves—a class too much despised to be feared; but between the whites and the free mulattos there was sufficient hatred to cause an outbreak at any moment, which might entail the most disastrous consequences.

During the first days of August a strange incident occurred, which threw a slight shade of uneasiness over the sunshine of my happiness.

CHAPTER III.

On the banks of a little river, which flowed through my uncle's estate, was a small rustic pavilion in the midst of a clump of trees.

Marie was in the habit of coming here every day to enjoy the sea breeze, which blows regularly in St. Domingo, even during the hottest months of the year, from sunrise until evening.

Each morning it was my pleasant task to adorn this charming retreat with the sweetest flowers that I could gather.

One morning Marie came running to me in a great state of alarm: upon entering her leafy retreat she had perceived, with surprise and terror, all the flowers which I had arranged in the morning thrown upon the ground and trampled underfoot, and a bunch of wild marigolds, freshly gathered, placed upon her accustomed seat. She had hardly recovered from her terror when, in the adjoining coppice, she heard the sound of a guitar, and a voice, which was not mine, commenced singing a Spanish song; but in her excitement she had been unable to catch the meaning of the words, though she could hear her own name frequently repeated. Then she had taken to flight, and had come to me full of this strange and surprising event.

This recital filled me with jealousy and indignation. My first suspicions pointed to the mulatto with whom I had fought; but, even in the midst of my perplexity, I resolved to do nothing rashly. I soothed Marie's fears as best I could, and promised to watch over her without ceasing until the marriage tie would give me the right of never leaving her.

Believing that the intruder whose insolence had so alarmed Marie would not content himself with what he had already done, I concealed myself that very evening near the portion of the house in which my betrothed's chamber was situated.

Hidden amongst the tall stalks of the sugar-cane, and armed with a dagger, I waited; and I did not wait in vain. Towards the middle of the night my attention was suddenly attracted by the notes of a guitar under the very window of the room in which Marie reposed. Furious with rage, with my dagger clutched firmly in my hand, I rushed in the direction of the sound, crushing beneath my feet the brittle stalks of the sugar-canes. All of a sudden I felt myself seized and thrown upon my back with what appeared to be superhuman force, my dagger was wrenched from my grasp, and I saw its point shining above me; at the same moment I could perceive a pair of eyes and a double row of white teeth gleaming through the darkness, whilst a voice, in accents of concentrated rage, muttered, "*Te tengo, te tengo*" (I have you, I have you).

More astonished than frightened, I struggled vainly with my formidable antagonist, and already the point of the dagger had pierced my clothes, when Marie, whom the sound of the guitar and the noise of the struggle had aroused, appeared suddenly at her window. She recognized my voice, saw the gleam of the knife, and uttered a cry of terror and affright. This cry seemed to paralyze the hand of my opponent. He stopped as if petrified; but still, as though undecided, he kept the point of the dagger pressed upon my chest; then he suddenly exclaimed in French, "No, I cannot; she would weep too much," and, casting away the weapon, rose to his feet, and in an instant disappeared in the canes; and before I could rise, bruised and shaken from the struggle, no sound and no sign remained of the presence or the flight of my adversary.

It was some time before I could recover my scattered faculties. I was more furious than ever with my unknown rival, and was overcome with a feeling of shame at being indebted to him for my life.

"After all, however," I thought, "it is to Marie that I owe it; for it was the sound of *her* voice that caused him to drop his dagger."

And yet I could not hide from myself that there was something noble in the sentiment which had caused my unknown rival to spare me. But who could he be? One supposition after another rose in my mind, all to be discarded in turn. It could not be the mulatto planter to whom my suspicions had first been directed. He was not endowed with such muscular power; nor was it his voice. The man with whom I had struggled was naked to the waist. Slaves alone went about half-clothed in this manner. But this could not be a slave. The feeling which had caused him to throw away the dagger would not have been found in the bosom of a slave; and besides, my whole soul revolted at the idea of having a slave for a rival. What was to be done? I determined to wait and watch.

CHAPTER IV.

Marie had awakened her old nurse, whom she looked upon almost in the light of the mother who had died in giving her birth, and with them I remained for the rest of the night, and in the morning I informed my uncle of the mysterious occurrence. His surprise was extreme, but, like me, his pride would not permit him to believe that a slave would venture to raise his eyes to his daughter. The nurse received the strictest orders from my uncle never to leave Marie alone for a moment, but as the sittings of the Provincial Assembly, the threatening aspect of the affairs of the colony, and the superintendence of the plantation allowed him but little leisure, he authorized me to accompany his daughter whenever she left the house, until the celebration of our nuptials, and at the same time, presuming that the daring lover must be lurking in the neighbourhood, he ordered the boundaries of the plantation to be more strictly guarded than ever.

After all these precautions had been taken, I determined to put the matter to further proof. I returned to the summer-house by the river, and repairing the destruction of the evening before, I placed a quantity of fresh flowers in their accustomed place. When the time arrived at which Marie usually sought the sweet shades of this sequestered spot, I loaded my rifle and proposed to escort her thither. The old nurse followed a few steps behind.

Marie, to whom I had said nothing about my having set the place to rights, entered the summer-house the first. "See, Leopold," said she, "my nest is in the same condition in which I left it yesterday; here are your flowers thrown about in disorder and trampled to pieces, and there is that odious bouquet which does not appear at all faded since yesterday; indeed, it looks as if it had been freshly gathered."

I was speechless with rage and surprise. There was my morning's work utterly ruined, and the wild flowers, at whose freshness Marie was so much astonished, had insolently usurped the place of the roses that I had strewn all over the place.

"Calm yourself," said Marie, who noticed my agitation; "this insolent intruder will come here no more; let us put all thoughts of him on one side, as I do this nasty bunch of flowers."

I did not care to undeceive her, and to tell her that he *had* returned, yet I was pleased to see the air of innocent indignation with which she crushed the flowers under her foot, but hoping that the day would again come when I should meet my mysterious rival face to face, I made her sit down between her nurse and myself.

Scarcely had we done so than Marie put her finger on my lips; a sound, deadened by the breeze and the rippling of the stream, had struck upon her ear. I listened; it was the notes of a guitar, the same melody that had filled me with fury on the preceding evening. I made a movement to start from my seat, but a gesture of Marie's detained me.

"Leopold," whispered she, "restrain yourself, he is going to sing, and we shall learn who he is."

As she spoke, a few more notes were struck on the guitar, and then from the depths of the wood came the plaintive melody of a Spanish song, every word of which has remained deeply engraved on my memory.

Why dost thou fear me and fly me?
   Say, has my music no charms?
Do you not know that I love you?
   Why, then, these causeless alarms?
                   Maria!

When I perceive your slight figure
   Glide through the cocoa-nut grove
Sometimes I think 'tis a spirit
   Come to reply to my love.
                   Maria!

Sweeter your voice to mine ears
   Than the bird's song in the sky,
That from the kingdom I've lost,
   Over the wide ocean fly.
                   Maria!

Far away, once I was king,
   Noble, and powerful, and free;
All I would gladly give up
   For a word, for a gesture from thee,
                   Maria!

Tall and upright as a palm,
   Sweet in your young lover's eyes
As the soft shade of the tree
   Mirrored in cool water lies.
                   Maria!

But know you not that the storm
   Comes and uproots the fair tree?

Jealousy comes like that storm,
   Bringing destruction to thee,
               Maria!
Tremble, Hispaniola's daughter,
   Lest all should fade and decay;
And vainly you look for the arm
   To bear you in safety away.
               Maria!
Why, then, repulse my fond love?
   Black I am, whilst you are white;
Night and the day, when united,
   Bring forth the beautiful light.
               Maria!

CHAPTER V.

A prolonged quavering note upon the guitar, like a sob, concluded the song. I was beside myself with rage. King—black—slave! A thousand incoherent ideas were awakened by this extraordinary and mysterious song. A maddening desire to finish for once and all with this unknown being, who dared to mingle the name of Marie with songs of love and menace, took possession of me. I grasped my rifle convulsively and rushed from the summer-house. Marie stretched out her arms to detain me, but I was already in the thicket from which the voice appeared to have come. I searched the little wood thoroughly, I beat the bushes with the barrel of my rifle, I crept behind the trunks of the large trees, and walked through the high grass.

Nothing—nothing—always nothing! This fruitless search added fuel to the fire of my anger. Was this insolent rival always to escape from me like a supernatural being? Was I never to be able to find out who he was, or to meet him? At this moment the tinkling of bells roused me from my reverie. I turned sharply round, the dwarf Habibrah was at my side.

"Good day, master," said he, with a sidelong glance full of triumphant malice at the anxiety which was imprinted on my face.

"Tell me," exclaimed I, roughly, "have you seen any one about here?"

"No one except yourself, señor mio," answered he, calmly.

"Did you hear no voice?" continued I.

The slave remained silent, as though seeking for an evasive reply.

My passion burst forth. "Quick, quick!" I exclaimed. "Answer me quickly, wretch! did you hear a voice?"

He fixed his eyes boldly upon mine; they were small and round, and gleamed like those of a wild cat.

"What do you mean by a voice, master? There are voices everywhere—the voice of the birds, the voice of the stream, the voice of the wind in the trees——"

I shook him roughly. "Miserable buffoon," I cried, "cease your quibbling, or you shall hear another voice from the barrel of my rifle. Answer at once; did you hear a man singing a Spanish song?"

"Yes, señor," answered he, calmly. "Listen, and I will tell you all about it. I was walking on the outskirts of the wood listening to what the silver bells of my *gorra* (cap) were telling me, when the wind brought to my ears some Spanish words, the first language that I heard when my age could have been counted by months, and my mother carried me slung at her back in a hammock of red and yellow wool. I love the language, it recalls to me the time when I was little without being a dwarf, a little child, and not a buffoon; and so I listened to the song."

"Is that all that you have to say?" cried I, impatiently.

"Yes, handsome master; but if you like I can tell you what the man was who sang."

I felt inclined to clasp him in my arms.

"Oh, speak!" I exclaimed; "speak! here is my purse, and ten others fuller than that shall be yours if you will tell me his name."

He took the purse, opened it, and smiled.

"Ten purses fuller than this," murmured he; "that will make a fine heap of good gold coins; but do not be impatient, young master, I am going to tell you all. Do you remember the last verse of his song, something about 'I am black, and you are white, and the union of the two produces the beautiful light'? Well, if this song is true, Habibrah, your humble slave, was born of a negress and a white, and must be more beautiful than you, master; I am the offspring of day and night, therefore I am more beautiful than a white man, and——"

He accompanied this rhapsody with bursts of laughter.

"Enough of buffoonery," cried I; "tell me who was singing in the wood."

"Certainly, master, the man who sang such buffooneries, as you rightly term them, could only have been—a fool like me! Have I not gained my ten purses?"

I raised my hand to chastise his insolence, when a wild shriek rang through the wood from the direction of the summer-house.

It was Marie's voice.

Like an arrow I darted to the spot, wondering what fresh misfortune could be in store for us, and in a few moments arrived, out of breath, at the door of the pavilion. A terrible spectacle presented itself to my eyes.

An enormous alligator, whose body was half concealed by the reeds and water plants, had thrust his monstrous head through one of the leafy sides of the summer-house; his hideous widely opened mouth threatened a young negro of colossal height, who with one arm sustained Marie's fainting form, whilst with the other he had plunged the iron portion of a hoe between the sharp and pointed teeth of the monster. The reptile struggled fiercely against the bold and courageous hand that held him at bay.

As I appeared at the door, Marie uttered a cry of joy, and extricating herself from the support of the negro, threw herself into my arms with "I am saved, I am saved!" cried she.

At the movement and exclamation of Marie the negro turned abruptly round, crossed his arms on his breast, and casting a look of infinite sorrow upon my betrothed, remained immovable, taking no heed of the alligator, which, having freed itself from the hoe, was advancing on him in a threatening manner.

There would have been a speedy end of the courageous negro, had I not rapidly placed Marie on the knees of her nurse, who, more dead than alive, was gazing upon the scene, and, coming close to the monster, discharged my carbine into its yawning mouth. The huge reptile staggered back, its bleeding jaws opened and shut convulsively, its eyes closed, and after one or two unavailing efforts it rolled over upon its back, with its scaly feet stiffening in the air. It was dead. The negro whose life I had so happily preserved turned his head and saw the last convulsive struggles of the monster, then he fixed his eyes upon Marie, who had again cast herself into my arms, and in accents of the deepest despair, he exclaimed in Spanish, "Why did you kill him?" and, without waiting for a reply, leaped into the thicket and disappeared.

CHAPTER VI.

The terrible scene, its singular conclusion, the extraordinary mental emotions of every kind which had accompanied and followed my vain researches in the wood, had made my brain whirl. Marie was still stupefied with the danger that she had so narrowly escaped, and some time elapsed before we could frame coherent words, or express ourselves otherwise than by looks and clasping of the hands.

At last I broke the silence.

"Come, Marie, let us leave this, some fatality seems attached to the place."

She rose eagerly, as if she had only been waiting for my permission to do so, and, leaning upon my arm, we quitted the pavilion. I asked her how it had happened that succour had so opportunely arrived when the danger was so imminent, and if she knew who the slave was who had come to her assistance; for that it *was* a slave, was shown by his coarse linen trousers—a dress only worn by that unhappy class.

"The man," replied Marie, "is no doubt one of my father's negroes who was at work in the vicinity when the appearance of the alligator made me scream, and my cry must have warned him of my danger. All I know is, that he rushed out of the wood and came to my help."

"From which side did he come?" asked I.

"From the opposite side from which the song came, and into which you had just gone."

This statement upset the conclusion that I had been drawing from the Spanish words that the negro had addressed to me, and from the song in the same language by my unknown rival. But yet there was a crowd of other similarities. This negro of great height, and powerful muscular development, might well have been the adversary with whom I had struggled on the preceding night. In that case his half-clothed person would furnish a striking proof. The singer in the wood had said, "I am black"—a further proof.

He had declared himself to be a king, and this one was only a slave, but I recollected that in my brief examination I had been surprised at the noble appearance of his features, though of course accompanied by the characteristic signs of the African race.

The more that I thought of his appearance, the nobleness of his deportment, and his magnificent proportions, I felt that there might be some truth in his statement that he had been a king. But then came the crushing blow to my pride: if he had dared to gaze with an eye of affection upon Marie, if he had made her the object of his serenades, *he*, a *negro* and a *slave*, what punishment could be sufficiently severe for his presumption? With these thoughts all my indecision returned again, and again my anger increased against the mysterious unknown. But at the moment that these ideas filled my brain, Marie dissipated them entirely by exclaiming, in her gentle voice—

"My Leopold, we must seek out this brave negro, and pay him the debt of gratitude that we owe him, for without him I should have been lost, for you would have arrived too late."

These few words had a decisive effect; it did not alter my determination to seek out the slave, but it entirely altered the design with which I sought him, for it was to recompense and not to punish him that I was now eager.

My uncle learned from me that he owed his daughter's life to the courage of one of his slaves, and he promised me his liberty as soon as I could find him out.

CHAPTER VII.

Up to that time my feelings had restrained me from going into those portions of the plantation where the slaves were at work. It had been too painful for me to see so much suffering which I was powerless to alleviate. But on the day after the events had taken place which I have just narrated, upon my uncle asking me to accompany him on his tour of inspection, I accepted his proposal with eagerness, hoping to meet amongst the labourers the preserver of my much beloved Marie.

I had the opportunity in this visit of seeing how great a power the master exercises over his slaves, but at the same time I could perceive at what a cost this power was bought, for though at the presence of my uncle all redoubled their efforts, I could perceive that there was as much hatred as terror in the looks that they furtively cast upon him.

Irascible by temperament, my uncle seemed vexed at being unable to discover any object upon which to vent his wrath, until Habibrah the buffoon, who was ever at his heels, pointed out to him a young negro, who, overcome by heat and fatigue, had fallen asleep under a clump of date-trees.

My uncle stepped quickly up to him, shook him violently, and in angry tones ordered him to resume his work.

The terrified slave rose to his feet, and in so doing disclosed a Bengal rose-tree upon which he had accidentally laid, and which my uncle prized highly.

The shrub was entirely destroyed.

At this the master, already irritated at what he called the idleness of his slave, became furious. Foaming with rage, he unhooked from his belt the whip with wire plaited thongs, which he always carried with him on his rounds, and raised his arm to strike the negro who had fallen at his feet.

The whip did not fall.

I shall, as long as I live, never forget that moment. A powerful grasp arrested the hand of the angry planter, and a negro (it was the very one that I was in search of) exclaimed, "Punish me, for I *have* offended you, but do not hurt my brother who has but broken your rose-tree."

This unexpected interposition from the man to whom I owed Marie's safety, his manner, his look, and the haughty tone of his voice, struck me with surprise. But his generous intervention, far from causing my uncle to blush for his causeless anger, only increased the rage of the incensed master, and turned his anger upon the new-comer.

Exasperated to the highest pitch, my uncle disengaged his arm from the grasp of the tall negro, and pouring out a volley of threats, again raised the whip to strike him. This time, however, it was torn from his hand, and the negro, breaking the handle studded with iron nails as you would break a straw, cast it upon the ground and trampled upon the instrument of degrading punishment.

I was motionless with surprise, my uncle with rage, for it was an unheard-of thing for him to find his authority thus contemned. His eyes appeared ready to start from their sockets, and his lips quivered with passion.

The negro gazed upon him calmly, and then, with a dignified air, he offered him an axe that he held in his hand.

"White man," said he, "if you wish to strike me, at least take this axe."

My uncle, beside himself with rage, would certainly have complied with his request, for he stretched out his hand to grasp the dangerous weapon; but I in my turn interfered, and seizing the axe, threw it into the well of a sugar-mill which was close at hand.

"What have you done?" asked my uncle, angrily.

"I have saved you," answered I, "from the unhappiness of striking the preserver of your daughter; it is to this slave that you owe Marie; it is the negro to whom you have promised liberty."

It was an unfortunate moment in which to remind him of

his promise. My words could not soothe the wounded dignity of the planter.

"His liberty!" replied he, savagely. "Yes, he has deserved that an end should be put to his slavery; his liberty indeed! we shall see what sort of liberty the members of a court-martial will accord him."

These menacing words chilled my blood. In vain did Marie join her entreaties to mine.

The negro whose negligence had been the cause of this scene was punished with a severe flogging, whilst his defender was thrown into the dungeons of Fort Galifet, under the terrible accusation of having assaulted a white man; for a slave who did this, the punishment was invariably death.

CHAPTER VIII.

You may judge, gentlemen, how much all these circumstances excited my curiosity and interest. I made every inquiry regarding the prisoner, and some strange particulars came to my knowledge. I learned that all his comrades displayed the greatest respect for the young negro. Slave as he was, he had but to make a sign to be implicitly obeyed. He was not born upon the estate, nor did any one know his father or mother: all that was known of him was that some years ago, a slave ship had brought him to St. Domingo. This circumstance rendered the influence which he exercised over the slaves the more extraordinary, for, as a rule, the negroes born upon the island profess the greatest contempt for the *Congos*, a term which they apply to all slaves brought direct from Africa.

Although he seemed a prey to deep dejection, his enormous strength, combined with his great skill, rendered him very valuable in the plantation. He could turn more quickly, and for a longer period than a horse, the wheels of the sugar-mills, and often in a single day performed the work of ten of his companions to save them from the punishment which their negligence or incapacity had rendered them liable. For this reason he was adored by the slaves, but the respect that they paid him was of an entirely different character from the superstitious dread with which they looked upon Habibrah the Jester.

What was more strange was the modesty and gentleness with which he treated his equals, in contrast to the pride and haughtiness which he displayed to the negroes who acted as overseers. These privileged slaves, the intermediary links in the chain of servitude, too often exceed the little brief authority that is delegated to them, and find a cruel pleasure in overwhelming those beneath them with work. Not one of them, however, had ever dared to inflict any species of punishment on him, for had they done so, twenty negroes would have stepped forward to take his place, whilst he would have looked gravely on, as thought he considered that they were merely performing a duty. The strange being was known throughout the negro quarter as *Pierrot*.

CHAPTER IX.

The whole of these circumstances took a firm hold upon my youthful imagination. Marie, inspired by compassion and gratitude, applauded my enthusiasm, and Pierrot excited our interest so much, that I determined to visit him and offer him my services in extricating him from his perilous position. As the nephew of one of the richest colonists in the Cap, I was, in spite of my youth, a captain in the Acul Militia. This regiment, and a detachment of the Yellow Dragoons, had charge of Fort Galifet; the detachment was commanded by a non-commissioned officer, to whose brother I had once had the good fortune to render an important service, and who therefore was entirely devoted to me.

(Here the listeners at once pronounced the name of Thaddeus.)

You are right, gentlemen (replied the captain), and as you may well believe, I had not much trouble in penetrating to the cell in which the negro was confined. As a captain in the militia, I had of course the right to visit the fort; but to evade the suspicions of my uncle, whose rage was still unabated, I took care to go there at the time of his noonday *siesta*. All the soldiers too, except those on guard, were asleep, and guided by Thaddeus I came to the door of the cell. He opened it for me, and then discreetly retired.

The negro was seated on the ground, for, on account of

his height, he could not stand upright. He was not alone, an enormous dog was crouched at his feet, which rose with a growl, and moved toward me.

"Rask," cried the negro.

The dog ceased growling, and again laid down at his master's feet, and began eating some coarse food.

I was in uniform, and the daylight that came through the loophole in the wall of the cell was so feeble that Pierrot could not recognize my features.

"I am ready," said he, in a clear voice.

"I thought," remarked I, surprised at the ease with which he moved, "that you were in irons."

He kicked something that jingled.

"Irons; oh, I broke them."

There was something in the tone in which he uttered these words, that seemed to say, "I was not born to wear fetters."

I continued: "I did not know that they had permitted you to have a dog with you."

"They did not allow it; I brought him in."

I was more and more astonished. Three bolts closed the door on the outside, the loophole was scarcely six inches in width, and had two iron bars across it.

He seemed to divine my thoughts, and raising as nearly erect as the low roof would permit, he pulled out with ease a large stone placed under the loophole, removed the iron bars, and displayed an opening sufficiently large to permit two men to pass through. This opening looked upon a grove of bananas and cocoa-nut trees which covered the hill upon which the fort was built.

Surprise rendered me dumb; at that moment a ray of light

fell on my face. The prisoner started as if he had accidentally trodden upon a snake, and his head struck against the ceiling of the cell. A strange mixture of opposing feelings passed over his face—hatred, kindness, and astonishment were all mingled together; but recovering himself with an effort, his face once more became cold and calm, and he gazed upon me as if I was entirely unknown to him.

"I can live two days more without eating," said he.

I saw how thin he had become, and made a movement of horror.

He continued, "My dog will only eat from my hand, and had I not enlarged the loophole, poor Rask would have died of hunger. It is better that he should live, for I know that I am condemned to death."

"No," I said; "no, you shall not die of hunger."

He misunderstood me.

"Very well," answered he, with a bitter smile, "I could have lived two days yet without food, but I am ready: to-day is as good as to-morrow. Do not hurt Rask."

Then I understood what he meant when he said "I am ready." Accused of a crime the punishment of which was death, he believed that I had come to announce his immediate execution; and yet this man endowed with herculean strength, with all the avenues of escape open to him, had in a calm and childlike manner repeated "I am ready!"

"Do not hurt Rask," said he, once more.

I could restrain myself no longer.

"What!" I exclaimed, "not only do you take me for your executioner, but you think so meanly of my humanity, that you believe I would injure this poor dog, who has never done me any harm!"

His manner softened, and there was a slight tremor in his voice as he offered me his hand, saying,

"White man, pardon me, but I love my dog, and your race have cruelly injured me."

I embraced him, I clasped his hand, I did my best to undeceive him.

"Do you not know me?" asked I.

"I know that you are white, and that a negro is nothing in the eyes of men of your colour; besides you have injured me."

"In what manner?" exclaimed I, in surprise.

"Have you not twice saved my life?"

This strange accusation made me smile; he perceived it, and smiled bitterly.

"Yes, I know it too well: once you saved my life from an alligator, and once from a planter, and what is worse I am denied the right to hate you, I am very unhappy."

The strangeness of his language and of his ideas surprised me no longer; it was in harmony with himself.

"I owe more to you than you can owe to me. I owe you the life of Marie, of my betrothed."

He started as though he had received some terrible shock. "Marie!" repeated he in stilled tones, and his face fell in his hands which trembled violently, whilst his bosom rose and fell with heavy sighs.

I must confess that once again my suspicions were aroused, but this time there were no feelings of anger or jealousy. I was too near my happiness, and he was trembling upon the brink of death, so that I could not for a moment look upon him as a rival, and even had I done so, his forlorn condition would have excited my compassion and sympathy.

At last he raised his head.

"Go," said he; "do not thank me."

After a pause he added, "And yet my rank is as lofty as your own."

These last words roused my curiosity, I urged him to tell me of his position, and his sufferings, but he maintained an obstinate silence.

My proceedings, however, had touched his heart, and my entreaties appeared to have vanquished his distaste for life. He left his cell, and in a short time returned with some bananas and a large cocoa-nut. Then he reclosed the opening and began to eat. As we conversed, I remarked that he spoke French and Spanish with equal facility, and that his education had not been entirely neglected. He knew many Spanish songs, which he sang with great feeling. Altogether he was a mystery that I endeavoured in vain to solve, for he would give me no key to the riddle. At last, with regret, I was compelled to leave him, after having urged on my faithful Thaddeus to permit him every possible indulgence.

CHAPTER X.

Every day at the same hour I visited him. His position rendered me very uneasy, for in spite of all our prayers, my uncle obstinately refused to withdraw his complaint. I did not conceal my fears from Pierrot, who however listened to them with indifference.

Often Rask would come in with a large palm-leaf tied round his neck. His master would take it off, read some lines traced upon it in an unknown language, and then tear it up. I had ceased to question him in any matters connected with himself.

One day as I entered he took no notice of me, he was seated with his back to the door of the cell, and was whistling in melancholy mood the Spanish air, "Yo que soy contrabandista" ("A smuggler am I"). When he had completed it, he turned sharply round to me, and exclaimed—

"Brother, if you ever doubt me, promise that you will cast aside all suspicion on hearing me sing this air."

His look was earnest, and I promised what he asked, without noticing the words upon which he laid so much stress, *"If ever you doubt me."* He took the empty half of a cocoa-nut which he had brought in on the day of my first visit, and had preserved ever since, filled it which palm wine, begged me to put my lips to it, and then drank it off at a draught. From that day he always called me *brother.*

And now I began to cherish a hope of saving Pierrot's life. My uncle's anger had cooled down a little. The preparations for the festivities, connected with his daughter's wedding had caused his feelings to flow in gentle channels. Marie joined her entreaties to mine. Each day I pointed out to him that Pierrot had had no desire to insult him, but had merely interposed to prevent him from committing an act of perhaps too great severity; that the negro had at the risk of his life saved Marie from the alligator; and besides, Pierrot was the strongest of all his slaves (for now I sought to save his life not to obtain his liberty), that he was able to do the work of ten men, and that his single arm was sufficient to put the rollers of a sugar-mill in motion. My uncle listened to me calmly, and once or twice hinted that he might not follow up his complaint.

I did not say a word to the negro of the change that had taken place, hoping that I should soon be the messenger to announce to him his restoration to liberty.

What astonished me greatly was, that though he believed that he was under sentence of death, yet he made no effort to avail himself of the means of escape that lay in his power. I spoke to him of this.

"I am forced to remain," said he simply, "or they would think that I was afraid."

CHAPTER XI.

One morning Marie came to me, she was radiant with happiness, and upon her gentle face was a sweeter expression than even the joys of pure love could produce, for written upon it was the knowledge of a good deed.

"Listen," said she. "In three days we shall be married. We shall soon——"

I interrupted her.

"Do not say *soon*, Marie, when there is yet an interval of three days."

She blushed and smiled.

"Do not be foolish, Leopold," replied she. "An idea has struck me which has made me very happy. You know that yesterday

I went to town with my father to buy all sort's of things for our wedding. I only care for jewels because you say that they become me. I would give all my pearls for a single flower from the bouquet which that odious man with the marigolds destroyed. But that is not what I meant to say. My father wished to buy me everything that I admired, and amongst other things there was a *basquina* of Chinese satin embroidered with flowers, which I admired. It was very expensive. My father noticed that the dress had attracted my attention. As we were returning home, I begged him to promise me a boon after the manner of the knights of old—you know how he delights to be compared to them. He vowed on his honour that he would grant me whatever I asked, thinking of course that it was the *basquina* of Chinese satin; but no, it is Pierrot's pardon that I will ask for as my nuptial present."

I could not refrain from embracing her tenderly. My uncle's word was sacred, and whilst Marie ran to him to claim its fulfilment, I hastened to Fort Galifet to convey the glad news to Pierrot.

"Brother," exclaimed I, as I entered, "Rejoice, your life is safe; Marie has obtained it as a wedding present from her father."

The slave shuddered.

"Marie—wedding—my life! What reference have these things to each other?"

"It is very simple," answered I. "Marie, whose life you saved, is to be married——."

"To whom?" exclaimed the negro, a terrible change coming over his face.

"Did you not know that she was to be married to me?"

His features relaxed.

"Ah, yes," he replied; "and when is the marriage to take place?"

"On August the 22nd."

"On August the 22nd! Are you mad?" cried he, with terror painted in his countenance.

He stopped abruptly; I looked at him with astonishment. After a short pause he clasped my hand—

"Brother," said he, "I owe you so much that I must give you a warning. Trust to me, take up your residence in Cap, and get married before the 22nd."

In vain I entreated him to explain his mysterious wards.

"Farewell," said he, in solemn tones; "I have perhaps said too much, but I hate ingratitude even more than perjury."

I left the prison a prey to feelings of great uneasiness; but all these were soon effaced by the thoughts of my approaching happiness.

That very day my uncle withdrew his charge, and I returned to the Fort to release Pierrot. Thaddeus, on hearing the noise, accompanied me to the prisoner's cell, but he was gone! Rask alone remained, and came up to me wagging his tail. To his neck was fastened a palm-leaf, upon which were written these words: "Thanks; for the third time you have saved my life. Do not forget your promise, friend;" whilst underneath, in lieu of signature, were the words: "Yo que soy contrabandista."

Thaddeus was even more astonished than I was, for he was ignorant of the enlargement of the loophole, and firmly believed that the negro had changed himself into a dog. I allowed him to remain in this belief, contenting myself with making him promise to say nothing of what he had seen. I wished to take Rask home with me, but on leaving the Fort he plunged into a thicket and disappeared.

CHAPTER XII.

My uncle was furiously enraged at the escape of the negro. He ordered a diligent search to be made for him, and wrote to the Governor placing Pierrot entirely at his disposal should he be re-taken.

The 22nd of August arrived. My union with Maria was celebrated with every species of rejoicing at the parish church of Acul. How happily did that day commence from which all our misfortunes were to date!

I was intoxicated with my happiness, and Pierrot and his mysterious warning were entirely banished from my thoughts. At last the day came to a close, and my wife had retired to her apartments; but for a time duty forbade me joining her there. My position as a captain of militia required me that evening to make the round of the guards posted about Acul. This nightly precaution was absolutely necessary owing to the disturbed state of the colony, caused by occasional outbreaks amongst the negroes, which, however, had been promptly repressed. My uncle was the first to recall me to the recollection of my duty. I had no option but to yield, and, putting on my uniform, I went out. I visited the first few guards without discovering any cause of alarm; but towards midnight, as half buried in my own thoughts I was patrolling the shores of the bay, I perceived upon the horizon a ruddy light in the direction of Limonade and Saint Louis du Morin. At first my escort attributed it to some accidental conflagration; but in a few moments the flames became so vivid, and the smoke rising before the wind grew so thick, that I ordered an immediate return to the Fort to give the alarm, and to request that help might be sent in the direction of the fire.

In passing through the quarters of the negroes who belonged to our estate, I was surprised at the extreme disorder that reigned there. The majority of the slaves were afoot, and were talking together with great earnestness. One strange word was pronounced with the greatest respect—it was *Bug-Jargal*—and occurred continually in the almost unintelligible dialect that they used.

From a word or two which I gathered here and there, I learned that the negroes of the northern districts were in open revolt, and had set fire to the dwelling-houses and the plantations on the other side of Cap.

Passing through a marshy spot, I discovered a quantity of axes and other tools, which would serve as weapons, hidden amongst the reeds. My suspicions were now thoroughly aroused, and I ordered the whole of the Acul militia to get under arms, and gave the command to my lieutenant, and, whilst my poor Marie was expecting me, I, obeying my uncle's orders, who, as I have mentioned, was a member of the Provincial Assembly, took the road to Cap, with such soldiers as I had been able to muster. I shall never forget the appearance of the town as we approached. The flames from the plantations which were burning all around it, threw a lurid light upon the scene, which was only partially obscured by the clouds of smoke which the wind drove into the narrow streets. Immense masses of sparks rose from the burning heaps of sugar-cane, and fell like fiery snow on the roofs of the houses, and on the rigging of the vessels at anchor in the roadsteads, at every moment threatening the town of Cap with as serious a conflagration as was already raging in its immediate neighbourhood. It was a terrible sight to witness the terror-stricken inhabitants exposing their lives to preserve from so destructive a visitant their habitations, which perhaps was the last portion of property left to them; whilst, on the other hand, the vessels, taking advantage of a fair wind, and fearing the same fate, had already set sail, and were gliding over an ocean reddened by the flames of the conflagration.

CHAPTER XIII.

Stunned by the noise of the minute-guns from the Fort, by the cries of the fugitives, and the distant crash of falling buildings, I did not know in what direction to lead my men; but, meeting in the main square the captain of the Yellow Dragoons, he advised me to proceed direct to the Governor.

Other hands have painted the disasters of Cap, and I must pass quickly over my recollections of them, written as they are in fire and blood. I will content myself with saying that the insurgent slaves were already masters of Dondon, of Terrier-Rouge, of the town of Ouanaminte, and of the plantation of Limbé. This last news filled me with uneasiness, owing to the proximity of Limbé to Acul. I made all speed to the Government House. All was in confusion there. I asked for orders, and begged that instant measures might be taken for the security of Acul, which I feared the insurgents were already threatening. With the Governor, Monsieur de Blanchelande, were M. de Rouvray, the Brigadier, and one of the largest landholders in Cap; M. de Touzard, the Lieutenant-Colonel of the Regiment of Cap; a great many members of the Colonial and the Provincial Assemblies, and numbers of the leading colonists. As I entered, all were engaged in a confused argument.

"Your Excellency," said a member of the Provincial Assembly, "it is only too true, it is the negroes, and not the free mulattoes; it has often been pointed out that there was danger in that direction."

"You make that statement without believing in its truth," answered a member of the Colonial Assembly, bitterly, "and you only say it to gain credit at our expense. So far from expecting a rising of the slaves, you got up a sham one in 1789. A ridiculous farce in which with a supposed insurgent force of three thousand slaves, *one* national volunteer only was killed, and that most likely by his own comrades."

"I repeat," replied the *Provincial*, "that we can see farther than you. It is only natural. We remain upon the spot and study the minutest details of the colony, whilst you and your Assembly hurry off to France to make some absurd proposals; which are often met with a national reprimand *Ridiculus mus.*"

The member of the Colonial Assembly answered with a sneer—

"Our fellow citizens re-elected us all without hesitation."

"It was your Assembly," retorted the other, "that caused the execution of that poor devil who neglected to wear a tricolored cockade in a *café*, and who commenced a petition for capital punishment to be inflicted on the mulatto Lacombe with that worn-out phrase, 'In the name of the Father, of the Son, and the Holy Ghost.' "

"It is false," exclaimed the other; "there has always been a struggle of principles against privileges between our assemblies."

"Ha, Monsieur, I see now you are an *Independent*."

"That is tantamount to allowing that you are in favour of the *White Cockade*: I leave you to get out of that confession as best you may."

More might have passed, but the Governor interposed.

"Gentlemen, gentlemen, what has this to do with the present state of affairs, and the pressing danger that threatens us? Listen to the reports that I have received. The revolt began this night at ten o'clock amongst the slaves in the Turpin Plantation. The negroes, headed by an English slave named Bouckmann, were joined by the blacks from Clement, Trémés, Flaville, and Nöe. They set fire to all the plantations, and massacred the colonists with the most unheard-of barbarities. By one single detail I can make you comprehend all the horrors accompanying this insurrection. The standard of the insurgents is the body of a white child on the point of a pike."

A general cry of horror interrupted the Governor's statement.

"So much," continued he, "for what has passed outside the town. Within its limits all is confusion. Fear has rendered many of the inhabitants forgetful of the duties of humanity, and they have murdered their slaves. Nearly every one have confined their negroes behind bolts and bars. The white artisans accuse the free mulattoes of being participators in the revolt, and many have had great difficulty in escaping from the fury of the populace. I have had to grant them a place of refuge in a church, guarded by a regiment of soldiers; and now, to prove that they have nothing in common with the insurgents, they asked that they may be armed and led against the rebels."

"Do nothing of the kind, your Excellency," cried a voice which I recognized as that of the planter with whom I had had a duel. "Do nothing of the kind; give no arms to the mulattoes."

"What, do you not want to fight?" asked a planter, with a sneer.

The other did not appear to hear him, and continued: "These men of mixed blood are our worst enemies, and we must take every precaution against them. It is from that quarter that the insurgents are recruited; the negroes have but little to do with the rising." The poor wretch hoped by his abuse of the mulattoes to prove that he had nothing in common with them, and to clear himself from the imputation of having black blood in his veins; but the attempt was too barefaced, and a murmur of disgust rose up on all sides.

"Yes," said M. de Rouvray, "the slaves *have* something to do with it, for they are forty to one; and we should be in a serious plight if we could only oppose the negroes and the mulattoes with whites like you."

The planter bit his lips.

"General," said the Governor, "what answer shall be given to the petition: shall the mulattoes have the arms?"

"Give them weapons, your Excellency; let us make use of every willing hand. And you, sir," he added, turning to the colonist of doubtful colour. "Go arm yourself, and join your comrades."

The humiliated planter slunk away, filled with concentrated

rage.

But the cries of distress which rang through the town reached even to the chamber in which the council was being held. M. de Blanchelande hastily pencilled a few words upon a slip of paper, and handed it to one of his aides-de-camp, who at once left the room.

"Gentlemen, the mulattoes will receive arms; but there are many more questions to be settled."

"The Provincial Assembly should at once be convoked," said the planter who had been speaking when first I entered.

"The Provincial Assembly?" retorted his antagonist; "what is the Provincial Assembly?"

"You do not know because you are a member of the Colonial Assembly," replied the favourer of the *White Cockade.*

The *Independent* interrupted him. "I know no more of the Colonial than the Provincial—I only recognize the General Assembly."

"Gentlemen," exclaimed a planter, "whilst we are losing time with this nonsense, tell me what is to become of my cotton and my cochineal?"

"And my indigo at Lumbé?"

"And my negroes, for whom I paid twenty dollars a-head all round?" said the captain of a slave ship.

"Each minute that you waste," continued another colonist, "costs me ten quintals of sugar, which at seventeen piastres the quintal makes one hundred and thirty livres, ten sous, in French money, by the——"

Here the rival upholders of the two Assemblies again sought to renew their argument.

"Morbleu," said M. de Rouvray in a voice of thunder, striking the table violently, "what eternal talkers you are! What do we care about your two assemblies. Summon both of them, your Excellency, and I will form them into two regiments, and when they march against the negroes we shall see whether their tongues or their muskets make the most noise."

Then turning towards me he whispered—

"Between the two Assemblies and the Governor nothing can be done. These fine talkers spoil all, as they do in Paris. If I was seated in his Excellency's chair, I would throw all these fellows out of the window, and with my soldiers and a dozen crosses of St. Louis to promise, I would sweep away all the rebels in the island. These fictitious ideas of liberty, which they have all run mad after in France, do not do out here. Negroes should be treated so as not to upset them entirely by sudden liberation; all the terrible events of to-day are merely the result of this utterly mistaken policy, and this rising of the slaves is the natural result of the taking of the Bastille."

Whilst the old soldier thus explained to me his views—a little narrow-minded perhaps, but full of the frankness of conviction—the stormy argument was at its height. A certain planter, one amongst the few who were bitten with the rabid mania of the revolution, and who called himself Citizen General C——, because he had assisted at a few sanguinary executions, exclaimed—

"We must have punishments rather than battles. Every nation must exist by terrible examples; let us terrify the negroes. It was I who quieted the slaves during the risings of June and July by lining the approach to my house with a double row of negro heads. Let each one join me in this, and let us defend the entrances to Cap with the slaves who are still in our hands."

"How?" "What do you mean?" "Folly," "The height of imprudence," was heard on all sides.

"You do not understand me, gentlemen. Let us make a ring of negro heads, from Fort Picolet to Point Caracole. The rebels, their comrades, will not then dare to approach us. I have five hundred slaves who have remained faithful—I offer them at once."

This abominable proposal was received with a cry of horror.

"It is infamous! It is too disgusting!" was repeated by at least a dozen voices.

"Extreme steps of this sort have brought us to the verge of destruction," said a planter. "If the execution of the insurgents of June and July had not been so hurried on, we should have held in our hands the clue to the conspiracy, which the axe of the executioner divided for ever."

Citizen C—— was silenced for a moment by this outburst; then in an injured tone he muttered—

"I did not think that *I*, above all others, should have been suspected of cruelty. Why, all my life I have been mixed up with the lovers of the negro race. I am in correspondence with Briscot and Pruneau de Pomme-Gouge, in France; with Hans Sloane, in England; with Magaw, in America; with Pezll, in Germany; with Olivarius, in Denmark; with Wadstiörn, in Sweden; with Peter Paulus, in Holland; with Avendaño, in Spain; and with the Abbé Pierre Tamburini, in Italy!"

His voice rose as he ran through the names of his correspondents amongst the lovers of the African race, and he terminated his speech with the contemptuous remark—

"But, after all, there are no true philosophers here."

For the third time M. de Blanchelande asked if any one had

anything further to propose.

"Your Excellency," cried one, "let us embark on board the *Leopard*, which lies at anchor off the quay."

"Let us put a price on the head of Bouckmann," exclaimed another.

"Send a report of what has taken place to the Governor of Jamaica," suggested a third.

"A good idea, so that he may again send us the ironical help of five hundred muskets!" sneered a member of the Provincial Assembly. "Your Excellency, let us send the news to France, and wait for a reply."

"Wait—a likely thing indeed," exclaimed M. de Rouvray; "and do you think that the blacks will wait, eh? And the flames that encircle our town, do you think that they will wait? Your Excellency, let the tocsin be sounded, and send dragoons and grenadiers in search of the main body of the rebels. Form a camp in the eastern division of the island; plant military posts at Trou and at Vallieres. I will take charge of the plain of Dauphin; but let us lose no more time, for the moment for action has arrived."

The bold and energetic speech of the veteran soldier hushed all differences of opinion. The general had acted wisely. That secret knowledge which every one possesses most conducive to his own interests, caused all to support the proposal of General de Rouvray; and whilst the Governor with a warm clasp of the hand showed his old friend that his counsels had been appreciated, though they had been given in rather a dictatorial manner, the colonists urged for the immediate carrying out of the proposals.

I seized the opportunity to obtain from M. de Blanchelande

the permission that I so ardently desired, and, leaving the room, mustered my company in order to return to Acul—though, with the exception of myself, all were worn out with the fatigue of their late march.

CHAPTER XIV.

Day began to break as I entered the market-place of the town, and began to rouse up the soldiers, who were lying about in all directions wrapped in their cloaks, and mingled pell-mell with the Red and Yellow Dragoons, fugitives from the country, cattle bellowing, and property of every description sent in for security by the planters. In the midst of all this confusion I began to pick out my men, when I saw a private in the Yellow Dragoons, covered with dust and perspiration, ride up at full speed. I hastened to meet him, and in a few broken words he informed me that my fears were realized—that the insurrection had spread to Acul, and that the negroes were besieging Fort Galifet, in which the planters and the militia had taken refuge. I must tell you that this fort was by no means a strong one, for in St. Domingo they dignify the slightest earthwork with the name of fort.

There was not a moment to be lost. I mounted as many of my soldiers as I could procure horses for, and taking the dragoon as a guide, I reached my uncle's plantation about ten o'clock. I scarcely cast a glance at the enormous estate, which was nothing but a sea of flame, over which hovered huge clouds of smoke, through which every now and then the wind bore trunks of trees covered with sparks. A terrible rustling and crackling sound seemed to reply to the distant yells of the negroes which we now began to hear, though we could not as yet see them. The destruction of all this wealth, which would eventually have become mine, did not cause me a moment's regret. All I thought of was the safety of Marie—what mattered anything else in the world to me? I knew that she had taken refuge in the fort, and I prayed to God that I might arrive in time to rescue her. This hope sustained me through all the anxiety I felt, and gave me the strength and courage of a lion. At length a turn in the road permitted us to see the fort. The tricolour yet floated on its walls, and a well-sustained fire was kept up by the garrison. I uttered a shout of joy. "Gallop, spur on!" said I to my men, and redoubling our pace we dashed across the fields in the direction of the scene of action.

Near the fort I could see my uncle's house; the doors and windows were dashed in, but the walls still stood, and shone red with the reflected glare of the flames, which, owing to the wind being in a contrary direction, had not yet reached the building.

A crowd of the insurgents had taken possession of the house, and showed themselves at the windows and on the roof. I could see the glare of torches and the gleam of pikes and axes, whilst a brisk fire of musketry was kept up on the fort.

Another strong body of negroes had placed ladders against the walls of the fort and strove to take it by assault, though many fell under the well-directed fire of the defenders.

These black men always returning to the charge after each repulse, looked like a swarm of ants endeavouring to scale the shell of a tortoise, and shaken off by each movement of the sluggish reptile.

We reached the outworks of the fort, our eyes fixed upon the banner which still floated above it. I called upon my men to remember that their wives and children were shut up within those walls, and I urged them to fly to their rescue. A general cheer was the reply, and, forming column, I was on the point of giving the order to charge, when a loud yell was heard, a cloud of smoke enveloped the fort, and for a time concealed it from our sight; a roar was heard like that of a furnace in full blast, and as it cleared away we saw a red flag floating proudly above the dismantled walls. All was over. Fort Galifet was in the hands of the insurgents.

CHAPTER XV.

I cannot tell you what my feelings were at this terrible spectacle. The fort was taken, its defenders slain, and twenty families massacred; but I confess, to my shame, that I thought not of this. Marie was lost to me—lost, after having been made mine but a few brief hours before. Lost, perhaps, through my fault, for had I not obeyed the orders of my uncle in going to Cap I should have been by her side to defend her, or at least to die with her. These thoughts raised my grief to madness, for my despair was born of remorse.

However, my men were maddened at the sight. With a shout of "Revenge," with sabres between their teeth and pistols in either hand, they burst into the ranks of the victorious insurgents. Although far superior in numbers the negroes fled at their approach; but we could see them on our right and left, before and behind us, slaughtering the colonists, and casting fuel on the flames. Our rage was increased by their cowardly conduct.

Thaddeus, covered with wounds, made his escape through a postern gate. "Captain," said he, "your Pierrot is a sorcerer, an *obi* as these infernal negroes call him—a devil, I say. We were holding our position, you were coming up fast; all seemed saved—when by some means, which I do not know, he penetrated into the fort, and there was an end of us. As for your uncle and Madam——"

"Marie," interrupted I, "where is Marie?"

At this instant a tall black burst through a blazing fence, carrying in his arms a young woman who shrieked and struggled: it was Marie, and the negro was Pierrot!

"Traitor," cried I.

I fired my pistol at him; one of the rebels threw himself in the way, and fell dead. Pierrot turned, and addressed a few words to me which I did not catch; and then grasping his prey tighter, dashed into a mass of burning sugar-canes. A moment afterwards a huge dog passed me, carrying in his mouth a cradle in which lay my uncle's youngest child. Transported with rage, I fired my second pistol at him; but it missed fire. Like a madman I followed on their tracks; but my night march, the hours that I had spent without taking rest or food, my fears for Marie, and the sudden fall from the height of happiness to the depth of misery, had worn me out. After a few steps I staggered, a cloud seemed to come over me, and I fell senseless.

CHAPTER XVI.

When I recovered my senses I found myself in my uncle's ruined house, supported in the arms of my faithful Thaddeus, who gazed upon me with an expression of the deepest anxiety. "Victory!" exclaimed he, as he felt my pulse begin to beat. "Victory! the negroes are in full retreat and my captain has come to life again."

I interrupted his exclamations of joy by putting the only question in which I had any interest.

"Where is Marie?"

I had not yet collected my scattered ideas: I felt my misfortune, without the recollection of it. At my question Thaddeus hung his head.

Then my memory returned to me, and, like a hideous dream, I recalled once more the terrible nuptial day, and the tall negro bearing away Marie through the flames.

The flame of rebellion which had broken out in the colony caused the whites to look on the blacks as their mortal enemies, and made me see in Pierrot, the good, the generous, and the devoted, who owed his life three times to me, a monster of ingratitude and a rival.

The carrying off of my wife on the very night of our nuptials proved too plainly to me, what I had at first only suspected, and I now knew that the singer of the wood was the wretch who had torn my wife from me. In a few hours how great a change had taken place.

Thaddeus told me that he had vainly pursued Pierrot and his dog when the negroes, in spite of their numbers, retired, and that the destruction of my uncle's property still continued, without the possibility of its being arrested.

I asked what had become of my uncle. He took my hand in silence and led me to a bed, the curtains of which he drew.

My unhappy uncle was there, stretched upon his blood-stained couch, with a dagger driven deeply into his heart. By the tranquil expression of his face it was easy to see that the blow had been struck during his sleep.

The bed of the dwarf Habibrah, who always slept at the foot of his master's couch, was also profusely stained with gore, and the same crimson traces could be seen upon the laced coat of the poor fool, cast upon the floor a few paces from the bed.

I did not hesitate for a moment in believing that the dwarf had died a victim to his affection for my uncle, and that he had been murdered by his comrades, perhaps in the effort to defend his master. I reproached myself bitterly for the prejudice which had caused me to form so erroneous an estimate of the characters of Pierrot and Habibrah; and of the tears I shed at the tragic fate of my uncle, some were dedicated to the end of the faithful fool.

By my orders his body was carefully searched for, but all in vain, and I imagined that the negroes had cast the body into the flames; and I gave instructions that, in the funeral service over my uncle's remains, prayers should be said for the repose of the soul of the devoted Habibrah.

CHAPTER XVII.

Fort Galifet had been destroyed, our house was in ruins; it was useless to linger there any longer, so that evening I returned to Cap. On my arrival there I was seized with a severe fever. The effort that I had made to overcome my despair had been too violent; the spring had been bent too far and had snapped. Delirium came on. My broken hopes, my profound love, my lost future, and, above all, the torments of jealousy, made my brain reel.

It seemed as if fire flowed in my veins; my head seemed ready to burst, and my bosom was filled with rage. I pictured to myself Marie in the arms of another lover, subject to the power of a master, of a slave, of Pierrot! They told me afterwards that I sprang from my bed, and that it took six men to prevent me from dashing out my brains against the wall. Why did I not die then?

The crisis, however, passed. The doctors, the care and attention of Thaddeus, and the latent powers of youth, conquered the malady; would that it had not done so. At the end of ten days I was sufficiently recovered to lay aside grief, and to live for vengeance.

Hardly arrived at a state of convalescence, I went to M. de Blanchelande, and asked for employment. At first he wished to give me the command of some fortified post, but I begged him to attach me to one of the flying columns, which from time to time were sent out to sweep those districts in which the insurgents had congregated. Cap had been hastily put in a position of defence, for the revolt had made terrible progress, and the negroes of Port au Prince had begun to show symptoms of disaffection. Biassou was in command of the insurgents at Lumbé, Dondon, and Acul; Jean François had proclaimed himself generalissimo of the rebels of Maribarou, and Bouckmann, whose tragic fate afterwards gave him a certain celebrity, with his brigands ravaged the plains of Limonade; and lastly, the bands of Morne-Rouge had elected for their chief a negro called Bug-Jargal.

If report was to be believed, the disposition of this man contrasted very favourably with the ferocity of the other chiefs. Whilst Bouckmann and Biassou invented a thousand different methods of death for such prisoners as fell into their hands, Bug-Jargal was always ready to supply them with the means of quitting the island. M. Colas de Marjue, and eight other distinguished colonists, were by his orders released from the terrible death of the wheel to which Bouckmann had condemned them, and many other instances of his humanity were cited, which I have not time to repeat.

My hoped for vengeance, however, still appeared to be far removed. I could hear nothing of Pierrot. The insurgents commanded by Biassou continued to give us trouble at Cap; they had once even endeavoured to take position on a hill that commanded the town, and had only been dislodged by the battery from the citadel being directed upon them.

The Governor had therefore determined to drive them into the interior of the island. The militia of Acul, of Lumbé, of Ouanaminte, and of Maribarou, joined with the regiment of Cap, and the Red and Yellow Dragoons, formed one army of attack; whilst the corps of volunteers under the command of the merchant Poncignon, with the militia of Dondon and Quartier-Dauphin, composed the garrison of the town.

The Governor desired first to free himself from Bug-Jargal, whose incursions kept the garrison constantly on the alert, and he sent against him the militia of Ouanaminte, and a battalion of the regiment of Cap. Two days afterwards the expedition returned, having sustained a severe defeat at the hands of Bug-Jargal. The Governor, however, determined to persevere, and a fresh column was sent out with fifty of the Yellow Dragoons and four hundred of the militia of Maribarou. This second expedition met with even less success than the first. Thaddeus, who had taken part in it, was in a violent fury, and upon his return vowed vengeance against the rebel chief Bug-Jargal.

*   *   *   *   *   *

A tear glistened in the eyes of D'Auverney; he crossed his arms on his breast, and appeared to be for a few moments plunged in a melancholy reverie. At length he continued.

CHAPTER XVIII.

The news had reached us that Bug-Jargal had left Morne-Rouge, and was moving through the mountains to effect a junction with the troops of Biassou. The Governor could not conceal his delight. "We have them," cried he, rubbing his hands. "They are in our power."

By the next morning the colonial forces had marched some four miles to the front of Cap. At our approach the insurgents hastily retired from the positions which they had occupied at Port-Mayat and Fort Galifet, and in which they had planted siege guns which they had captured in one of the batteries on the coast. The Governor was triumphant, and by his orders we continued our advance. As we passed through the arid plains and the ruined plantations, many a one cast an eager glance in search of the spot which was once his home, but in too many cases the foot of the destroyer had left no traces behind. Sometimes our march was interrupted by the conflagration having spread from the lands under cultivation, to the virgin forests.

In these regions, where the land is untilled and the vegetation abundant, the burning of a forest is accompanied with many strange phenomena. Far off, long before the eye can catch the cause, a sound is heard like the rush of a cataract over opposing rocks, the trunks of the trees flame out with a sudden crash, the branches crackle, and the roots beneath the soil all contribute to the extraordinary uproar. The lakes and the marshes in the interior of the forests boil with the heat. The hoarse roar of the coming flame stills the air, causing a dull sound, sometimes increasing and sometimes diminishing in intensity as the conflagration sweeps on or recedes. Occasionally a glimpse can be caught of a clump of trees surrounded by a belt of fire, but as yet untouched by the flames; then a narrow streak of fire curls round the stems, and in another instant the whole becomes one mass of gold-coloured fire; then up rises the column of smoke driven here and there by the breeze. It takes a thousand fantastic forms, spreads itself out, diminishes in an instant; at one moment it is gone, in another it returns with greater density; then all becomes a thick black cloud, with a fringe of sparks, a terrible sound is heard, the sparks disappear, and the smoke ascends, disappearing at last in a mass of red ashes, which sink down slowly upon the blackened ground.

CHAPTER XIX.

On the evening of the third day of our march, we entered the ravines of Grande-Riviere; we calculated that the negro army was some twenty leagues off in the mountains.

We pitched our camp on a low hill, which appeared to have been used for the same purpose before, as the grass had been trodden down and the brushwood cut away. It was not a judicious position in a strategical point of view, but we deemed ourselves perfectly secure from attack. The hill was commanded on all sides by steep mountains clothed with thick forests—the precipitous sides of these hills had given the mountains the name of the *Dompté-Mulâtre*. The Grande-Riviere flowed behind our camp; confined within steep banks, it was just about here very deep and rapid. The sides were hidden with thickets, through which nothing could be seen. The waters of the stream itself were frequently concealed by masses of creeping plants, hanging from the branches of the flowering maples, which had sprung up at intervals in the jungle, crossing and recrossing the stream, and forming a tangled net-work of living verdure. From the heights of the adjacent hills they appeared like meadows still fresh with dew, whilst every now and then a dull splash could be heard as a teal plunged through the flower-decked curtain, and showed in which direction the river lay. By degrees the sun ceased to gild the crested peaks of the distant mountains of Dondon; little by little darkness spread its mantle over the camp, and the silence was only broken by the cry of the night-bird, or by the measured tread of the sentinels.

Suddenly the dreaded war-songs of "*Oua-Nassé*" and of "The Camp of the Great Meadow" were heard above our heads; the palms, the acomas, and the cedars, which crowned the summits of the rocks, burst into flames, and the lurid light of the conflagration showed us numerous bands of negroes and mulattoes, whose copper-hued skins glowed red in the firelight upon the neighbouring hills. It was the army of Biassou.

The danger was imminent. The officers, aroused from their sleep, endeavoured to rally their men. The drum beat the "Assembly," whilst the bugles sounded the "Alarm." Our men fell in hurriedly and in confusion; but the insurgents, instead of taking advantage of our disorder, remained motionless, gazing upon us, and continuing their song of "*Oua-Nassé.*"

A gigantic negro appeared alone on one of the peaks that overhung the Grande-Riviere, a flame-coloured plume floated on his head; he held an axe in his right hand and a blood-red banner in his left.

I recognized Pierrot.

Had a carbine been within my reach I should have fired at him, cowardly although the act might have been.

The negro repeated the chorus of "*Oua-Nassé,*" planted his

standard on the highest portion of the rock, hurled his axe into the midst of our ranks, and plunged into the stream. A feeling of regret seized me; I had hoped to have slain him with my own hand.

Then the negroes began to hurl huge masses of rocks upon us, whilst showers of bullets and flights of arrows were poured upon our camp. Our soldiers, maddened at being unable to reach their adversaries, fell on all sides, crushed by the rocks, riddled with bullets, and transfixed by arrows.

The army was rapidly falling into disorder.

Suddenly a terrible noise came from the centre of the stream.

The Yellow Dragoons, who had suffered most from the shower of rocks, had conceived the idea of taking refuge under the thick roof of creepers which grew over the river. It was Thaddeus who had at first discovered this——

Here the narrative was suddenly interrupted.

CHAPTER XX.

More than a quarter of a hour had elapsed since Thaddeus, his arm in a sling, had glided into the tent without any of the listeners noticing his arrival, and, taking up his position in a remote corner, he had by occasional gestures expressed the interest that he took in his captain's narrative; but at last, considering that this direct allusion to himself ought not to be permitted to pass without some acknowledgement on his part, he stammered out—

"You are too good, captain."

A general burst of laughter followed this speech, and D'Auverney, turning towards him, exclaimed severely—

"What, Thaddeus, you here?—and your arm?"

On being addressed in so unaccustomed a tone, the features of the old soldier grew dark; he quivered, and threw back his head, as though to restrain the tears which seemed to struggle to his eyes.

"I never thought," said he, in a low voice, "that you, captain, could have omitted to say *thou* when speaking to your old sergeant."

"Pardon me, old friend," answered the captain, quickly; "I hardly knew what I said. Thou wilt pardon me, wilt thou not?"

The tears sprang to the sergeant's eyes in spite of his efforts to repress them.

"It is the third time," remarked he—"but these are tears of joy."

Peace was made, and a short silence ensued.

"But tell me, Thaddeus, why hast thou quitted the hospital to come here?" asked D'Auverney, gently.

"It was—with your permission, captain—to ask if I should put the laced saddle-cloth on the charger for to-morrow."

Henri laughed. "You would have been wiser, Thaddeus, to have asked the surgeon-major if you should put two more pieces of lint on your arm," said he.

"Or to ask," continued Paschal, "if you might take a glass of wine to refresh yourself. At any rate, here is some brandy; taste it—it will do you good, my brave sergeant."

Thaddeus advanced, saluted, and, apologizing for taking the glass with his left hand, emptied it to the health of the assembled company.

"You had got, captain, to the moment when—yes, I remember, it was I who proposed to take shelter under the creepers, to prevent our men being smashed by the rocks. Our officer, who did not know how to swim, was afraid of being drowned, and, as was natural, was dead against it until he saw—with your permission, gentlemen—a great rock fall on the creepers without being able to get through them. 'It is better to die like Pharaoh than like St. Stephen,' said he: 'for we are not saints, and Pharaoh was a soldier like ourselves.' The officer was a learned man, you see. And so he agreed to my proposal, on the condition that I should first try the experiment myself. Off I went; I slid down the bank and caught hold of the roof of creepers, when all of a sudden some one took a pull at my legs. I struggled, I shouted for help, and in a minute I received half a dozen sabre cuts. Down came the dragoons to help me, and there was a nice little skirmish under the creepers. The blacks of Morne-Rouge had hidden themselves there, never for a moment thinking that we should fall right on the top of them. This was not the right time for fishing, I can tell you. We fought, we swore, we shouted. They had nothing particular on, and were able to move about in the water more easily than we were; but, on the other hand, our sabres had less to cut through. We swam with one hand and fought with the other. Those who could not swim, like my captain, hung on to the creepers, whilst the negroes pulled them by the legs. In the midst of the hullabaloo I saw a big negro fighting like Beelzebub against five or six of ours. I swam up to him, and I recognized Pierrot, otherwise called Bug——But I mustn't tell that yet, must I, captain? Since the capture of the fort I owed him a grudge, so I took him hard and fast by the throat; he was going to rid himself of me by a thrust of his dagger, when he recognized me, and gave himself up at once. That was very unfortunate, was it not, captain? for if he had not surrendered, he would not——But you will know that later on, eh? When the blacks saw that he was taken they made a rush at me to get him off; when Pierrot, seeing no doubt that they would all lose their lives, said some gibberish or other, and in the twinkling of an eye they plunged into the water, and were out of sight in a moment. This fight in the water would have been pleasant enough if I had not lost a finger, and wetted ten cartridges, and if the poor man——but it was to be, was it not, captain?"

And the sergeant respectfully placed the back of his hand to his forage cap, and then raised it to heaven with the air of an inspired prophet.

D'Auverney was violently agitated.

"Yes," cried he, "thou art right, my old Thaddeus; that night was a fatal night for me."

He would have fallen into one of his usual reveries had they not urgently pressed him to conclude his story.

After a while he continued.

CHAPTER XXI.

Whilst the scene which Thaddeus has just described was passing behind the camp, I had succeeded with some of my men in climbing the opposite hills, by aid of the brushwood, until we had reached a point called Peacock Peak, from the brilliant tints of the mica which coated the surface of the rock.

From this position, which was opposite a rock covered with negroes, we opened a withering fire. The insurgents, who were not so well armed as we were, could not reply warmly to our volleys, and in a short time began to grow discouraged. We redoubled our efforts, and our enemies soon evacuated the neighbouring rocks, first hurling the dead bodies of their comrades upon our army, the greater proportion of which was still drawn up on the hill. Then we cut down several trees, and binding the trunks together with fibres of the palm, we improvised a bridge, and by it crossed over to the deserted positions of the enemy, and thus managed to secure a good post of vantage. This operation completely quenched the courage of the rebels. Our fire continued. Shouts of grief arose from them, in which the name of Bug-Jargal was frequently repeated. Many negroes of the army of Morne-Rouge appeared on the rock upon which the blood-red banner still floated; they prostrated themselves before it, tore it from its resting-place, and then precipitated it and themselves into the depths of the Grande-Riviere. This seemed to signify that their chief was either killed or a prisoner.

Our confidence had now risen to such a pitch that I resolved to drive them from their last position at the point of the bayonet, and at the head of my men I dashed into the midst of the negroes. The soldiers were about to follow me across the temporary bridge that I had caused to be thrown from peak to peak, when one of the rebels with a blow of his axe broke the bridge to atoms, and the ruins fell into the abyss with a terrible noise.

I turned my head—in a moment I was surrounded, and seized by six or seven negroes, who disarmed me in a moment. I struggled like a lion, but they bound me with cords made of bark, heedless of the hail of bullets that my soldiers poured upon them.

My despair was somewhat soothed by the cries of victory which I heard from our men, and I soon saw the negroes and mulattoes ascending the steep sides of the rocks with all the precipitation of fear, uttering cries of terror.

My captors followed their example. The strongest amongst them placed me on their shoulders, and carried me in the direction of the forest, leaping from rock to rock with the agility of wild goats. The flames soon ceased to light the scene, and it was by the pale rays of the moon that we pursued our course.

CHAPTER XXII.

After passing through jungle, and crossing many a torrent, we arrived in a valley situated in the higher part of the hills, of a singular wild and savage appearance. The spot was absolutely unknown to me. The valley was situated in the heart of the hills, in what is called the *double mountains*. It was a large green plain, imprisoned by walls of bare rock, and dotted with clumps of pines and palm-trees. The cold, which at this height is very severe, was increased by the morning air, the day having just commenced to break, but the valley was still plunged in darkness, and was only lighted by flashes from the negroes' fires; evidently this spot was their headquarters. The shattered remains of their army had begun to reassemble, and every now and then bands of negroes and mulattoes arrived, uttering groans of distress and cries of rage. New fires were speedily lighted, and the camp began to increase in size. The negro whose prisoner I was had placed me at the foot of an oak, whence I surveyed this strange spectacle with entire carelessness. The black had bound me with his belt to the trunk of the tree, against which I was leaning, and carefully tightening the knots in the cords which impeded my movements, he placed on my head his own red woollen cap, as if to indicate that I was his property, and after making sure that I could not escape or be carried off by others, was preparing to leave me, when I determined to address him, and speaking in the Creole dialect I asked him if he belonged to the band of Dondon, or of Morne-Rouge. He stopped at once, and in a tone of pride replied *"Morne-Rouge."* Then an idea entered my head. I had often heard of the generosity of the chief Bug-Jargal, and though I had made up my mind that death would soon end all my troubles, yet the thought of the tortures that would inevitably precede it should I fall into the hands of Biassou, filled me with horror. All I wanted was to be put to death without torment. It was perhaps a weakness, but I believe that the mind of man ever revolts at such a death. I thought then, that if I could be taken from Biassou, Bug-Jargal might give me what I desired—a soldier's death. I therefore asked the negro of Morne-Rouge to lead me to Bug-Jargal. He started. "Bug-Jargal," he repeated, striking on his forehead in anguish; then, as if rage had suddenly overtaken him, he shook his fist, and shouting "Biassou, Biassou," he left me hastily.

The mingled rage and grief of the negro recalled to my mind the events of the day, and the certainty we had acquired of either the death or capture of the chief of the band of Morne-Rouge. I felt that all hope was over, and resigned myself to the threatened vengeance of Biassou.

CHAPTER XXIII.

A group of negresses came near the tree to which I was fastened, and lit a fire. By the numerous bracelets of blue, red, and violet glass which ornamented their arms and ankles, by the rings which weighed down their ears and adorned their toes and fingers, by the amulets on their bosoms and the collar of charms suspended round their necks, and by the aprons of variegated feathers which were their sole coverings, I at once recognized them as *griotes*. You are perhaps ignorant that amongst the African blacks there exists a certain class with a rude talent for poetry and improvisation, which approaches closely to madness. These unhappy creatures, wandering from one African kingdom to another, are in these barbarian countries looked upon in the same light as the *minstrels* of England, the *minnesingers* of Germany, and the *troubadours* of France. They are called *griots*, and their wives *griotes*. The *griotes* accompany the barbaric songs of their husbands with lascivious dances, and form a grotesque parody on the *nautch girls* of India and the *almes* of Egypt. It was a group of these women who came and sat down near me, with their legs crossed under them according to their custom, and their hideous faces lighted up by the red light of a fire of withered branches. When they had formed a complete circle they all took hands, and the eldest, who had a heron's plume stuck in her hair, began to exclaim "*Ouanga*." I at once understood that they were going through one of their performances of pretended witchcraft. Then the leader of the band, after a moment's silence, plucked a lock of hair from her head and threw it into the fire, crying out these words, "Malé o guiab," which in the jargon of the Creoles means, "I shall go to the devil." All the *griotes* imitated their leader, and throwing locks of their hair in the fire, repeated gravely, "Malé o guiab." This strange invocation, and the extraordinary grimaces that accompanied it, caused me to burst into one of those hysterical fits of laughter which so often seize on one even at the most serious moments. It was in vain that I endeavoured to restrain it—it would have vent; and this laugh which escaped from so sad a heart brought about a gloomy and terrifying scene.

Disturbed in their incantations, the negresses sprang to their feet. Until then they had not noticed me, but now they rushed close up to me, screaming "Blanco, Blanco." I have never seen so hideous a collection of faces, contorted as they were with passion, their white teeth gleaming, and their eyes almost starting from their heads. They were, I believe, about to tear me to pieces, when the old woman with the beaver's plume on her head stopped them with a sign of her hand, and exclaimed seven times, "Zoté cordé!" ("Do you agree?") The wretched creatures stopped at once, and, to my surprise, tore off their feather aprons, which they flung upon the ground, and commenced the lascivious dance which the negroes call "*La chica.*"

This dance, which should only consist of attitudes and movements expressive of gaiety and pleasure, assumed a very different complexion when performed by these naked sorceresses. In turn, each of them would place her face close to mine, and, with a frightful expression of countenance, would detail the horrible punishment that awaited the white man who had profaned the mysteries of their *Ouanga*.

I recollected that savage nations had a custom of dancing round the victims that they were about to sacrifice, and I patiently awaited the conclusion of the performance which I knew would be sealed with my blood; and yet I could not repress a shudder as I perceived each *griote*, in strict unison with the time, thrust into the fire the point of a sabre, the blade of an axe, a long sail-maker's needle, a pair of pincers, and the teeth of a saw.

The dance was approaching its conclusion, and the instruments of torture were glowing red with heat.

At a signal from the old woman, each negress in turn withdrew an implement from the fire, whilst those who had none furnished themselves with a blazing stick. Then I understood clearly what my punishment was to be, and that in each of the dancers I should find an executioner. Again the word of command was given, and the last figure of the dance was commenced. I closed my eyes that I might not see the frantic evolutions of these female demons, who, in measured cadence, clashed the red-hot weapons over their heads. A dull, clinking sound followed, whilst the sparks flew out in myriads. I waited, nerving myself for the moment when I should feel my flesh quiver in agony, my bones calcine, and my muscles writhe under the burning tortures of the nippers and the saws. It was an awful moment. Fortunately it did not last long.

In the distance I heard the voice of the negro whose prisoner I was, shouting, "*Que haceis, mujeres, ne demonio, que haceis alli, devais mi prisonero?*" I opened my eyes again; it was already broad daylight. The negro hurried towards me, gesticulating angrily. The *griotes* paused, but they seemed less influenced by the threats of my captor than by the presence of a strange-looking person by whom the negro was accompanied.

It was a very stout and very short man—a species of dwarf—whose face was entirely concealed by a white veil, pierced with three holes for the eyes and mouth. The veil hung down to his shoulders, and displayed a hairy, copper-hued breast, upon which was hung by a golden chain the mutilated sun of a monstrance.

The cross-hilt of a heavy dagger peeped from a scarlet belt, which also supported a kind of petticoat striped with green, yellow, and black, the hem of which hung down to his large and ill-shaped feet.

His arms, like his breast, were bare; he carried a white staff, and a rosary of amber beads was suspended from his belt, in close proximity to the handle of his dagger. His head was surmounted by a pointed cap adorned with bells, and when he came close I was not surprised in recognizing in it the *gorra* of Habibrah; and amongst the hieroglyphics with which it was covered, I could see many spots of gore: without doubt, it was the blood of the faithful fool. These bloodstains gave me fresh proofs of his death, and awakened in me once again a fresh feeling of regret for his loss.

Directly the *griotes* recognized the wearer of Habibrah's cap, they cried out all at once, "The Obi," and prostrated themselves before him. I guessed at once that this was a sorcerer attached to Biassou's force.

"Basta, basta" ("enough"), said he, in a grave and solemn voice, as he came close up to them. "Devais el prisonero de Biassou" ("Let the prisoner be taken to Biassou").

All the negresses leapt to their feet and cast their implements of torture on one side, put on their aprons, and, at a gesture of the Obi, fled like a cloud of grasshoppers.

At this instant the glance of the Obi fell upon me. He started back a pace, and half waved his white staff in the direction of the retiring *griotes*, as if he wished to recall them; then, muttering between his teeth the word "*Maldicho*" ("accursed"), he whispered a few words in the ear of the negro, and, crossing his arms, retired slowly, apparently buried in deep thought.

CHAPTER XXIV.

My captor informed me that Biassou had asked to see me, and that in an hour I should be brought before him. This, I calculated, gave me another hour in which to live. Until that time had elapsed, I allowed my glances to wander over the rebel camp, the singular appearance of which the daylight permitted me to observe. Had I been in any other position, I should have laughed heartily at the ostentatious vanity of the negroes, who were nearly all decked out in fragments of clerical and military dress, the spoils of their victims. The greater portion of these ornaments were not new, consisting of torn and blood-stained rags. A gorget could often be seen shining over a stole, whilst an epaulet looked strange when contrasted with a chasuble.

To make amends for former years of toil, the negroes remained in a state of utter inaction: some of them slept exposed to the rays of the sun, their heads close to a burning fire; others, with eyes that were sometimes full of listlessness, and at others blazed with fury, sat chanting a monotonous air at the doors of their *ajoupas*—a species of hut with conical roofs somewhat resembling our artillery tents, but thatched with palm or banana leaves.

Their black or copper-coloured wives, aided by the negro-children, prepared the food for the fighting-men. I could see them stirring up with long forks, ignames, bananas, yams, peas, cocus and maize, and other vegetables indigenous to the country, which boiled with joints of pork, turtle, and dog in the great boilers stolen from the dwellings of the planters. In the distance, on the outskirts of the camp, the *griots* and *griotes* formed large circles round the fires, and the wind every now and then brought to my ears strange fragments of their barbaric songs, mingled with notes from their tambourines and guitars. A few videttes posted on the high ground watched over the headquarters of the General Biassou: the only defence of which in case of attack was a circle of waggons filled with plunder and ammunition. These black sentries posted on the summits of the granite pyramids, with which the valley bristled, turned about like the weathercocks in Gothic spires, and with all the strength of their lungs shouted one to the other the cry of "*Nada, nada*" ("Nothing, nothing"), which showed that the camp was in full security. Every now and then groups of negroes, inspired by curiosity, collected round me, but all looked upon me with a threatening expression of countenance.

CHAPTER XXV.

At length an escort of negro soldiers very fairly equipped arrived. The negro whose property I appeared to be, unfastened me from the oak to which I was bound, and handed me over to the escort, receiving in exchange a bag full of piastres. As he lay upon the grass counting them with every appearance of delight, I was led away by the soldiers. My escort wore a uniform of coarse cloth, of a reddish-brown colour, with yellow facings; their head-dress was a Spanish cap called a*montera*, ornamented with a large red cockade. Instead of a cartouche case, they had a species of game-bag slung at their sides. Their arms were a heavy musket, a sabre, and a dagger. I afterwards learned that these men formed the body-guard of Biassou.

After a circuitous route through the rows of *ajoupas*, which were scattered all over the place, I came to a cave which nature had hollowed out in one of those masses of rock with which the meadow was full. A large curtain of some material from the looms of Thibet, which the negroes called *Katchmir*, and which is remarkable less for the brilliancy of its colouring than for the softness of its material, concealed the interior of the cavern from the vulgar gaze. The entrance was guarded by a double line of negroes, dressed like those who had escorted me thither.

After the countersign had been exchanged with the sentries who marched backwards and forwards before the cave, the commander of the escort raised the curtain sufficiently for me to enter, and then let it drop behind me. A copper lamp with six lights hung by a chain from the roof of the grotto, casting a flickering light upon the damp walls. Between the ranks of mulatto soldiers I perceived a coloured man sitting upon a large block of mahogany, which was partially covered with a carpet made of parrots' feathers. His dress was of the most absurd kind. A splendid silk girdle, from which hung a cross of Saint Louis, held up a pair of common blue trousers, whilst a waistcoat of white linen which did not meet the waistband of the trousers completed the strange costume. He wore high boots, and a round hat with a red cockade, and epaulets, one of gold with silver stars like those worn by brigadiers, whilst the other was of red worsted with two copper stars, which seemed to have been taken from a pair of spurs, fixed upon it, evidently to render it more worthy of its resplendent neighbour. A sabre and a pair of richly chased pistols lay by his side.

Behind the throne were two white children dressed in the costume of slaves, bearing large fans of peacock feathers.

Two squares of crimson velvet, which seemed to have been stolen from some church, were placed on either side of the mahogany block. One of these was occupied by the Obi who had rescued me from the frenzy of the *griotes*. He was seated with his legs crossed under him, holding in his hand his white wand; and not moving a muscle, he looked like a porcelain idol in a Chinese pagoda, but through the holes in his veil I could see his flashing eyes fixed steadfastly upon mine.

Upon each side of the general were trophies of flags, banners, and pennons of all kinds; among them I noticed the white flag with the lilies, the tricolour, and the banner of Spain. The others were covered with fancy devices. I also perceived a large standard entirely black.

At the end of the grotto, I saw a portrait of the mulatto Ogé who, together with his lieutenant Jean Charanne, had been broken on the wheel the year previous, for the crime of rebellion. Twenty of his accomplices, blacks and mulattoes, suffered with him.

In this painting Ogé, the son of a butcher at Cap, was represented in the uniform of a lieutenant-colonel, and decorated with the star of St. Louis, and the Order of Merit of the Lion, which last he had purchased from the Prince of Limburg.

The negro general into whose presence I had been introduced was short and of vulgar aspect, whilst his face showed a strange mixture of cunning and cruelty. After looking at me for some time in silence, with a bitter omen on his face, he said—

"I am Biassou."

I expected this, but I could not hear it from his mouth, distorted as it was by a cruel smile, without an inward trembling; but my face remained unchanged, and I made no reply.

"Well," continued he, in his bad French, "have they already impaled you, that you are unable to bend before Biassou, generalissimo of this conquered land, and brigadier of His Most Catholic Majesty?" (The rebel chiefs sometimes affected to be acting for the King of France, sometimes for the Republic, and at others for the King of Spain.)

I crossed my arms upon my chest, and looked him firmly in the face.

He again sneered. "Ho, ho," said he, "*me pareces hombre de buen corazon* ("You seem a courageous man"); well, listen to my questions. Were you born in the island?"

"No, I am a Frenchman."

My calmness irritated him.

"All the better; I see by your uniform that you are an officer. How old are you?"

"Twenty."

"When were you twenty?"

To this question, which aroused in me all the recollection of my misery, I could not at first find words to reply. He repeated it imperiously.

"The day upon which Leogri was hung," answered I.

An expression of rage passed over his face as he answered,

"It is twenty-three days since Leogri was executed. Frenchman, when you meet him this evening you may tell him from me that you lived twenty-four days longer than he did. I will spare you for to-day, I wish you to tell him of the liberty that his brethren have gained, and what you have seen at the headquarters of General Jean Biassou."

Then he ordered me to sit down in one corner between two of his guards, and with a motion of his hand to some of his men, who wore the uniform of aide-de-camps, he said,

"Let the assembly be sounded, that we may inspect the whole of our troops; and you, your Reverence," he added, turning to the Obi, "put on your priestly vestments, and perform for our army the holy sacrament of the Mass."

The Obi rose, bowed profoundly, and whispered a word or two in the general's ear.

"What," cried the latter, "no altar! but never mind, the good

Giu has no need of a magnificent temple for His worship. Gideon and Joshua adored Him before masses of rock, let us do as they did; all that is required is that the hearts should be true. No altar, you say—why not make one of that great chest of sugar which we took yesterday from Dubussion's house?"

This suggestion of Biassou was promptly carried into execution. In an instant the interior of the cave was arranged for a burlesque of the divine ceremony. A pyx and a monstrance stolen from the parish church of Acul were promptly produced (the very church in which my nuptials with Marie had been celebrated, and where we had received heaven's blessing which had so soon changed to a curse).

The stolen chest of sugar was speedily made into an altar and covered with a white cloth, through which, however, the words Dubussion and Company for Nantes could be plainly perceived.

When the sacred vessels had been placed on the altar, the Obi perceived that the crucifix was wanting. He drew his dagger which had a cross handle, and stuck it into the wood of the case in front of the pyx. Then without removing his cap or veil, he threw the cope which had been stolen from the priest of Acul over his shoulders and bare chest, opened the missal with its silver clasps from which the prayers had been read on my ill-fated marriage day; and turning towards Biassou, whose seat was a few paces from the altar, announced to him that all was ready.

On a sign from the general the Katchmir curtains were drawn aside, and the insurgent army was seen drawn up in close column before the entrance to the grotto.

Biassou removed his hat and knelt before the altar.

"On your knees," he cried, in a loud voice.

"On your knees!" repeated the commander of the battalions.

The drums were beaten, and all the insurgents fell upon their knees.

I alone refused to move, disgusted at this vile profanation about to be enacted under my very eyes; but the two powerful mulattoes who guarded me pulled my seat from under me, and pressed heavily upon my shoulders so that I fell on my knees, compelled to pay a semblance of respect to this parody of a religious ceremony. The Obi performed his duties with affected solemnity, whilst the two white pages of Biassou officiated as deacon and sub-deacon. The insurgents, prostrated before the altar, assisted at the ceremony with the greatest enthusiasm, the general setting the example.

At the moment of the exaltation of the host, the Obi, raising in his hands the consecrated vessel, exclaimed in his Creole jargon,

"Zoté coné bon Giu; ce li mo fé zoté voer. Blan touyé li, touyé blan yo toute!" ("You see your good God; I am showing Him to you. The white men killed Him; kill all the whites!")

At these words, pronounced in a loud voice, the tones of which had something in them familiar to my ear, all the rebels uttered a loud shout, and clashed their weapons together. Had it not been for Biassou's influence that hour would have been my last. To such atrocities may men be driven who use the dagger for a cross, and upon whose mind the most trivial event makes a deep and profound impression.

CHAPTER XXVI.

At the termination of the ceremony the Obi bowed respectfully to Biassou; then the general rose and, addressing me in French, said—

"We are accused of having no religion. You see it is a falsehood, and that we are good Catholics."

I do not know whether he spoke ironically or in good faith. A few moments he called for a glass bowl filled with grains of black maize; on the top he threw some white maize, then he raised it high in his hand so that all the army might see it.

"Brothers," cried he, "you are the black maize; your enemies are the white maize."

With these words he shook the bowl, and in an instant the white grains had disappeared beneath the black; and, as though inspired, he cried out, "Where are the white now?"

The mountains re-echoed with the shouts with which the illustration of the general was received; and Biassou continued his harangue, mixing up French, Creole dialect, and Spanish alternately.

"The season for temporising has passed; for a long time we have been as patient as the sheep to whose wool the whites compare our hair; let us now be as implacable as the panthers or the tigers of the countries from which they have torn us. Force alone can obtain for us our rights, and everything can be obtained by those who use their force without pity. Saint

Loup (Wolf) has two days in the year consecrated to him in the Gregorian calendar whilst the Paschal Lamb has but one. Am not I correct, your reverence?"

The Obi bowed in sign of corroboration.

"They have come," continued Biassou, "these enemies of ours have come as enemies of the regeneration of humanity; these whites, these planters, these men of business, veritable devils vomited from the mouth of hell. They came in the insolence of their pride, in their fine dresses, their uniforms, their feathers, their magnificent arms; they despised us because we were black and naked in their overbearing haughtiness; they thought that they could drive us before them as easily as these peacock's feathers disperse the swarms of sandflies and mosquitoes."

As he uttered these concluding words, he snatched from the hands of his white slaves one of the large fans, and waved it over his head with a thousand eccentric gesticulations. Then he continued—

"But, my brethren, we burst upon them like flies upon a carcase; they have fallen in their fine uniforms beneath the strokes of our naked arms, which they believed to be without power, ignorant that good wood is the stronger when the bark is stripped off; and now these accursed tyrants tremble, and are filled with fear."

A triumphant yell rose in answer to the general's speech, and all the army repeated, "They are filled with fear."

"Blacks, Creoles, and Congos," added Biassou, "vengeance and liberty! Mulattoes, do not be led away by the temptations of the white men. Your fathers serve in their ranks, but your mothers are with us; besides, 'O bermanos de mi alma' ('O brethren of my soul'), have they ever acted as fathers to you?

Have they not rather been cruel masters, and treated you as slaves, because you had the blood of your mothers in your veins? Whilst a miserable cotton garment covered your bodies scorched by the sun, your cruel fathers went about in straw hats and nankeen clothes on work days, and in cloth and velvet on holidays and feasts. Curses be on their unnatural hearts. But as the holy commandments forbid you to strike your father, abstain from doing so; but in the day of battle what hinders you from turning to your comrade and saying, 'Touyé papa moé, ma touyé quena toué?' ('Kill my father, and I will kill yours?') Vengeance then, my brethren, and liberty for all men. This cry has found an echo in every part of the island; it has roused Tobago and Cuba. It was Bouckmann, a negro from Jamaica, the leader of the twenty-five fugitive slaves of the Blue Mountain, who raised the standard of revolt amongst us. A glorious victory was the first proof that he gave of his brotherhood with the negroes of Saint Domingo. Let us follow his noble example, with an axe in one hand and a torch in the other. No mercy for the whites, no mercy for the planters; let us massacre their families, and destroy their plantations! Do not allow a tree to remain standing on their estates; let us upturn the very earth itself that it may swallow up our white oppressors! Courage then, friends and brethren; we shall fight them and sweep them from the face of the earth. We will conquer or die. As victors, we shall enjoy all the pleasures of life; and if we fall, the saints are ready to receive us in heaven, where each warrior will receive a double ration of brandy, and a silver piastre each day!"

This warlike discourse, which to you appears perfectly ridiculous, had a tremendous effect on the insurgents. It is true that Biassou's wild gesticulations, the manner in which his voice rose and fell, and the strange sneer which every now and then appeared on his lips, imparted to his speech a strange amount of power and fascination. The skill with which he alluded to those points which would have the greatest weight with the negroes, added a degree of force which told well with his audience.

I will not attempt to describe to you the outburst of determined enthusiasm which the harangue of Biassou roused amongst the rebels.

There arose at once a discordant chorus of howls, yells, and shouts. Some beat their naked breasts, others dashed their clubs and sabres together. Many threw themselves on their knees, and remained in that position as though in rapt ecstasy. The negresses tore their breasts and arms with their fish-bone combs. The sounds of drums, tom-toms, guitars, and tambourines were mingled with the discharge of firearms. It was a veritable witches' Sabbath.

Biassou raised his hand, and, as if by enchantment, the tumult was stilled, and each negro returned to his place in the ranks in silence. The discipline which Biassou had imposed upon his equals by the exercise of his power of will struck me, I may say, with admiration. All the soldiers of the force seemed to exist only to obey the wishes of their chief, as the notes of the harpsichord under the fingers of the musician.

CHAPTER XXVII.

The spectacle of another example of the powers of fascination and deception now attracted my attention, this was the healing of the wounded. The Obi, who in the army performed the double functions of healer of souls and bodies, began his inspection of his patients.

He had taken off his sacerdotal robes, and was seated before a large box in which he kept his drugs and instruments. He used the latter very rarely, but occasionally drew blood skilfully enough with a lancet made of fish-bone, but he appeared to me to use the knife which in his hands replaced the scalpel rather clumsily. In most cases he contented himself with prescribing orange flower water, or sarsaparilla, and a mouthful of old rum. His favourite remedy, however, and one which he said was an infallible panacea for all ills, was composed of three glasses of red wine in which was some grated nutmeg and the yolk of an egg boiled hard. He employed this specific for almost every malady. You will understand that his knowledge of medicine was as great a farce as his pretended religion, and it is probable that the small number of cures that he effected would not have secured the confidence of the negroes had he not had recourse to all sorts of mummeries and incantations, and acted as much upon their imaginations as upon their bodies. Thus, he never examined their wounds without performing some mysterious signs, whilst at other times he skilfully mingled together religion and negro superstition, and would put into their wounds a little *fetish* stone wrapped in a morsel of lint, and the patient would credit the stone with the healing effects of the lint. If any one came to announce to him the death of a patient he would answer solemnly, "I foresaw it; he was a traitor; in the burning of such and such a house he spared a white man's life; his death was a judgment." And the wondering crowd of rebels applauded him as he thus increased their deadly hatred for their adversaries. This impostor, amongst other methods, employed one which amused me by its singularity. One of the negro chiefs had been badly wounded in the last action. The Obi examined the wound attentively, dressed it as well as he was able, then, mounting the altar, exclaimed, "All this is nothing." He then tore two or three leaves from the missal, burnt them to ashes, and mingling them with some wine in the sacramental cup, cried to the wounded man, "Drink; this is the true remedy." The patient, stupidly fixing his eyes on the impostor, drank, whilst the Obi with raised hands seemed to call down blessings on his head, and it may be the conviction that he was healed brought about his cure.

CHAPTER XXVIII.

Another scene in which the Obi also played the principal part succeeded to this. The physician had taken the place of the priest, and the sorcerer now replaced the physician.

"Listen, men!" cried the Obi, leaping with incredible agility upon the improvised altar, and sinking down with his legs crossed under his striped petticoat. "Listen; who will dive into the book of fate? I can foretell the future. '*He estudiado la cienca de los Gitanos*' ('I have studied the sciences of the gipsies')."

A crowd of mulattoes and negroes hurriedly crowded up to him.

"One by one," said the Obi, in that voice which called to my mind some remembrances that I could not quite collect. "If you come all together, altogether you will enter the tomb."

They stopped. Just then a coloured man dressed in a white jacket and trousers, with a bandana handkerchief tied round his head, entered the cave. Consternation was depicted on his countenance.

"Well, Rigaud," said the general, "what is it?"

Rigaud, sometimes called General Rigaud, was the head of the mulatto insurgents at Lagu. A man who concealed much cunning under an appearance of candour, and cruelty beneath the mask of humanity. I looked upon him with much attention.

"General," whispered Rigaud, but as I was close to them I could catch every word, "on the outskirts of the camp there is a messenger from Jean François who has brought the news that Bouckmann has been killed in a battle with the whites under M. de Touzard, and that his head has been set upon the gates of the town as a trophy."

"Is that all?" asked Biassou, his eyes sparkling with delight at learning the diminution of the number of chiefs and the consequent increase of his own importance.

"The emissary of Jean François has in addition a message for you."

"That is all right," replied the general; "but get rid of this air of alarm, my good Rigaud."

"But," said Rigaud, "do you not fear the effect that the death of Bouckmann will have on the army?"

"You wish to appear more simple than you are, but you shall see what Biassou will do. Keep the messenger back for a quarter of an hour and all will go well."

Then he approached the Obi, who during this conversation had been exercising his functions as fortune-teller, questioning the wondering negroes, examining the lines on their hands and foreheads, and distributing more or less good luck according to the size and colour of the piece of money thrown by each negro into a silver-gilt basin which stood on one side. Biassou whispered a few words in his ear, and without making any reply the Obi continued his prophetic observations.

"He," cried the Obi, "who has in the middle of his forehead a little square or triangular figure will make a large fortune without work or toil. The figure of three interlaced S's on the forehead is a fatal sign; he who has it will certainly be drowned if he does not carefully avoid water. Four lines from the top of the nose, and turning round two by two towards the eyes, announces that you will be taken prisoner, and for a long time languish in a foreign prison."

Here the Obi paused.

"Friends," continued he, "I have observed this sign in the forehead of Bug-Jargal, the brave chief of Morne-Rouge."

These words, which convinced me that Bug-Jargal had been made prisoner, were followed by a cry of grief from a band of negroes who wore short scarlet breeches. They belonged to the band of Morne-Rouge.

Then the Obi began again—

"If you have on the right side of the forehead in the line of the moon a mark resembling a fork, do not remain idle, and avoid dissipation of all kinds. A small mark like the Arabic cypher 3 in the line of the sun betokens blows with a stick."

An old negro here interrupted the magician, and dragging himself to his feet begged him to dress his wound. He had been wounded in the face, and one of his eyes almost torn from the socket hung upon his cheek. The Obi had forgotten him when going through his patients. Directly, however, he saw him he cried out—

"Round marks on the right side of the forehead in the line of the moon foretell misfortunes to the sight. My man, let me see your hand."

"Alas, excellent sir," answered the other, "it is my eye that I want you to look at."

"Old man," replied the Obi, crossly, "it is not necessary to see your eye, give me your hand, I say."

The miserable wretch obeyed, moaning, "My eye, my eye."

"Good," cried the Obi; "if you see on the line of life a spot surrounded by a circle you will lose an eye. There is the mark. You will become blind of an eye."

"I am so already," answered the negro, piteously.

But the Obi had merged the physician in the sorcerer, and thrusting him roughly on one side continued—

"Listen, my men. If the seven lines on the forehead are slight, twisted, and lightly marked, they announce a short life. He who has between his eyebrows on the line of the moon the figure of two crossed arrows will be killed in battle. If the line of life which intersects the hand has a cross at its junction it foretells death on the scaffold, and here I must tell you, my brethren," said the Obi, interrupting himself, "that one of the bravest defenders of our liberties, Bouckmann, has all these fatal marks."

At these words all the negroes held their breath, and gazed on the impostor with glances of stupid admiration.

"Only," continued the Obi, "I cannot reconcile the two opposing signs, death on the battle-field and also on the scaffold, and yet my science is infallible."

He stopped and cast a meaning glance at Biassou, who whispered something to an officer, who at once quitted the cavern.

"A gaping mouth," continued the Obi, turning on his audience a malicious glance, "a slouching carriage, and arms hanging down by the side, announces natural stupidity, emptiness, and want of reasoning powers."

Biassou gave a sneer of delight; at that moment the aide-de-camp returned, bringing with him a negro covered with mud and dust, whose feet, wounded by the roots and flints, showed that he had just come off a long journey.

This was the messenger whose arrival Rigaud had announced. He held in one hand a letter, and in the other a document sealed with the design of a flaming heart. Round it was a monogram, composed of the letters M and N interlaced, no doubt intended as an emblem of the union of the free mulattos and the negro slaves. Underneath I could read this motto, "Prejudice conquered, the rod of iron broken, long live the king!" This document was a safe conduct given by Jean François.

The messenger handed his letter to Biassou, who hastily tore it open and perused the contents, then with an appearance of deep grief he exclaimed, "My brothers!" All bowed respectfully.

"My brothers, this is a despatch to Jean Biassou, generalissimo of the conquered states, Brigadier-General of His Catholic Majesty, from Jean François, Grand Admiral of France, Lieutenant-General of the army of the King of Spain and the Indies.

"Bouckmann, chief of the hundred and twenty negroes of the Blue Mountain, whose liberty was recognized by the Governor-General of Belle Combe, has fallen in the glorious struggle of liberty and humanity against tyranny and barbarism. This gallant chief has been slain in an action with the white brigands of the infamous Touzard. The monsters have cut off his head, and have announced their intention of exposing it on a scaffold in the main square of the town of Cap. Vengeance!"

A gloomy silence succeeded the reading of this despatch; but the Obi leapt on his altar, and waving his white wand, exclaimed in accents of triumph—

"Solomon, Zerobabel, Eleazar Thaleb, Cardau, Judas Bowtharicht, Avenoes, Albert the Great, Bohabdil, Jean de Hagul, Anna Baratio, Daniel Ogromof, Rachel Flintz, Allornino, I give you thanks. The science of the spirits has not deceived me; sons, friends, brothers, boys, children, mothers, all of you listen to me. What was it that I predicted? the marks on the forehead of Bouckmann announced that his life would be a short one, that he would die in battle, and that he would appear on the scaffold. The revelations of my art have turned out true to the letter, and those points which seemed the most obscure are now the most plain. Brethren, wonder and admire!"

The panic of the negroes changed during this discourse to a sort of admiring terror. They listened to the Obi with a species of confidence mingled with fear, whilst the latter, carried away by his own enthusiasm, walked up and down the sugar case, which presented plenty of space for his short steps.

A sneer passed over Biassou's face as he addressed the Obi.

"Your reverence, since you know what is to come, will you be good enough to tell me the future of Jean Biassou, Brigadier-General?"

The Obi halted on the top of his strange altar, which the credulity of the negroes looked upon as something divine, and answered, *"Venga vuestra merced"* ("Come, your Excellency"). At this moment the Obi was the most important man in the army; the military power bowed to the spiritual.

"Your hand, general?" said the Obi, stooping to grasp it. *"Empezo"* ("I begin"). The line of junction equally marked in its full length promises you riches and happiness; the line of life strongly developed announces a life exempt from ills, and a happy old age. Its narrowness shows your wisdom and your superior talents, as well as the generosity of your heart; and, lastly, I see what chiromancers call the luckiest of all signs, a number of little wrinkles in the shape of a tree with its branches extending upwards, this promises health and wealth, it also prognosticates courage. General, it curves in the direction of the little finger, this is the sign of wholesome severity."

As he said this the eyes of the Obi glanced at me through the apertures of his veil, and I fancied that I could catch a well-known voice under the habitual gravity of his intonation, as he continued—

"The line of health, marked with a number of small circles, announces that you will have, for the sake of the cause, to order a number of executions; divided here by a half-moon, shows that you will be exposed to great danger from ferocious beasts, that is to say, from the whites, if you do not exterminate them. The line of fortune surrounded, like the line of life, by little branches rising towards the upper part of the hand, confirms the position of power and supremacy to which you have been called; turning to the right, it is a symbol of your administrative capacity. The fifth line, that of the triangle prolonged to the root of the middle finger, promises you success in all your undertakings. Let me see your fingers: the thumb marked with little lines from the point to the nail shows that you will receive a noble heritage, that of the glory of the unfortunate Bouckmann, no doubt," added the Obi, in a loud voice. "The slight swelling at the root of the forefinger, lightly marked with lines, promises honours and dignities. The middle finger shows nothing. Your little finger is covered with lines crossing each other, you will vanquish all your enemies, and rise high above your rivals. These lines form the cross of Saint Andrew, a mark of genius and foresight. I also notice the figure of a circle, another token of your arrival at the highest power and dignity. 'Happy the man,' says Eleazar Thaleb, 'who possesses all these signs. Destiny has its choicest gifts in store for him, and his fortunate star announces the talent which will bring him glory.' And now, general, let me look at your forehead? 'He,' says Rachel Flintz, of Bohemia, 'who bears on his forehead, on the line of the sun, a square or a triangular mark, will make a great fortune.' Here is another prediction, 'If the mark is on the right, it refers to an important succession;' that of Bouckmann is, of course, again referred to. The mark in the shape of a horseshoe between the eyebrows, on the line of the moon, means that prompt vengeance will be taken for insult and tyranny. I have this mark as well as you."

The curious manner in which the Obi uttered these words, "I have this mark," attracted my attention.

"The mark of a lion's claw which you have on your left eyelid is only noticeable amongst men of undoubted courage; but to close this, General Jean Biassou, your forehead shows every sign of the most unexampled success, and on it is a combination of lines which form the letter M, the commencement of the name of the Blessed Virgin. In whatever part of the forehead, and in whatever line of the face, such a sign appears, the signification is the same—genius, glory, and power. He who bears it will always bring success to whatever cause he embraces, and those under his command will never have to regret any loss. He alone is worth all the soldiers of his army. You, general, are the elect of Fate."

"Thanks, your reverence," said Biassou, preparing to return to his mahogany throne.

"Stay a moment, general," said the Obi, "I forgot one last sign: the line of the sun, which is so strongly marked on your forehead, proves that you understand the way of the world, that you possess the wish to make others happy, that you have much liberality, and like to do things in a magnificent manner."

Biassou at once recognized his forgetfulness, and drawing from his pocket a heavy purse, he threw it into the plate, so as to prove that the line of the sun never lies.

But this miraculous horoscope of the general's had produced its effect upon the army. All the insurgents who, since the news of the death of Bouckmann attached greater weight than ever to the words of the Obi, lost their feelings of uneasiness and became violently enthusiastic, and trusting blindly in their infallible sorcerer and their predestined chief, began to shout, "Long live our Obi! long live our general!"

The Obi and Biassou glanced at each other, and I almost thought I could hear the stifled laugh of the one replied to by the sardonic chuckle of the other. I do not know how it was, but this Obi tormented me dreadfully; I had a feeling that I had seen or heard him before, and I made up my mind to speak to him.

"Ho, Obi, your reverence, doctor, here!" cried I to him.

He turned sharply round.

"There is some one here whose lot you have not yet cast—it is mine."

He crossed his arms over the silver sun that covered his hairy breast, but he made no reply.

I continued, "I would gladly know what you prophesy with regard to my future, but your worthy comrades have taken my watch and my purse, and I suppose you will not give me a specimen of your skill for nothing?"

He advanced quickly to me, and muttered hoarsely in my ear—

"You deceive yourself, let me see your hand."

I gave it, looking fixedly at him; his eyes sparkled as he bent over my hand.

"If the line of life," said he, "is cut by two transverse lines, it is the sign of immediate death, your life will be a short one. If the line of health is not in the centre of the hand, and if there is only the line of life, and the line of fortune united so as to form an angle, a natural death cannot be looked for. Do not, therefore, look for a natural death! If the bottom of the forefinger has a long line cutting it, a violent death will be the result. Prepare yourself for a violent death!"

There was a ring of pleasure in his sepulchral voice as he thus announced my death, but I listened to him with contempt and indifference.

"Sorcerer," said I, with a disdainful smile, "you are skilful, for you are speaking of a certainty."

Once more he came closer to me.

"You doubt my science," cried he; "listen, then, once more. The severance of the line of the sun on your forehead shows me that you take an enemy for a friend, and a friend for an enemy."

These words seemed to refer to the treacherous Pierrot, whom I loved, but who had betrayed me, and to the faithful Habibrah, who I had hated, and whose blood-stained garments attested his fidelity and his devotion.

"What do you say?" exclaimed I.

"Listen until the end," continued the Obi. "I spoke of the future, listen to the past. The line of the moon on your forehead is slightly curved—that signifies that your wife has been carried off."

I trembled, and endeavoured to spring from my seat, but my guards held me back.

"You have but little patience," continued the sorcerer; "listen to the end. The little cross that cuts the extremity of that curve shows me all; your wife was carried off on the very night of your nuptials."

"Wretch," cried I, "you know where she is! Who are you?"

I strove again to free myself, and to tear away his veil, but I had to yield to numbers and to force, and I had the mortification of seeing the mysterious Obi move away repeating, "Do you believe me now? Prepare for immediate death."

CHAPTER XXIX.

As if to draw my attention from the perplexity into which I had been thrown by the strange scene that had just passed, a new and more terrible drama succeeded to the farce that had been played between Biassou and the Obi. Biassou had again taken his place upon his mahogany throne, whilst Rigaud and the Obi were seated on his right and left; the latter, with his arms crossed on his breast, seemed to have given himself up to deep thought. Biassou and Rigaud were chewing tobacco, and an aide-de-camp had just asked if he should order a general march past of the forces, when a tumultuous crowd of negroes, with hideous shouts, arrived at the entrance of the grotto. They had brought with them three white prisoners to be judged by Biassou, but what they desired was easily shown by the cries of "Muerte! Muerte!" "Death, death!" the latter, no doubt, emanating from the English negroes of Bouckmann's band, many of whom had by this time arrived to join the French and Spanish negroes of Biassou.

The general with a gesture of his hand commanded silence, and ordered the three captives to be brought to the entrance of the grotto. I recognized two of them with considerable surprise; one was the Citizen General C——, that philanthropist who was in correspondence with all the lovers of the negro race in different parts of the globe, and who had proposed so cruel a mode of suppressing the insurrection to the governor. The other was the planter of doubtful origin, who manifested so great a dislike to the mulattoes, amongst whom the whites insisted on classing him. The third appeared to belong to a section called "poor whites"—that is to say, white men who had to work for their living: he wore a leathern apron, and his sleeves were turned up to his elbows. All the prisoners had been taken at different times, endeavouring to hide themselves in the mountains.

The "poor white" was the first one that was questioned.

"Who are you?" asked Biassou.

"I am Jacques Belin, carpenter to the Hospital of the Fathers, at Cap."

Surprise and shame struggled for the mastery in the features of the general.

"Jacques Belin!" repeated he, biting his lips.

"Yes," replied the carpenter; "do you not recognize me?"

"Begin," retorted the general, furiously, "by recognizing *me* and saluting me."

"I do not salute *my slave*," replied the carpenter, sturdily.

"Your slave, wretch!" cried the general.

"Yes," replied the carpenter; "yes, I was your first master, you pretend not to recognize me, but remember, Jean Biassou, that I sold you for thirty piastres in the Saint Domingo slave market."

An expression of concentrated rage passed over Biassou's face.

"Well," continued the carpenter, "you appear ashamed of having worked for me; ought not Jean Biassou to feel proud of having belonged to Jacques Belin? Your mother, the old idiot, has often swept out my shop, but at last I sold her to the majordomo of the Hospital of the Fathers, and she was so old and decrepit, that he would only give me thirty-two livres and six sous for her. There is my history and yours, but it seems as if the negroes and the mulattoes are growing proud, and that you have forgotten the time when you served Master Jacques Belin, the carpenter of Cap, on your knees."

Biassou listened to him with that sardonic smile that gave him the appearance of a tiger.

"Good," said he; then turning to the negroes who had captured Belin, "get two trestles, two planks, and a saw, and take this man away. Jacques Belin, carpenter of Cap, thank me, for you shall have a true carpenter's death."

His sardonic laugh too fully explained the horrible punishment that he destined for the pride of his former master, but Jacques Belin did not blench, and turning proudly to Biassou, cried—

"Yes, I ought to thank you, for I bought you for thirty piastres, and I got work out of you to a much greater amount."

They dragged him away.

CHAPTER XXX.

More dead than alive, the other two prisoners had witnessed this frightful prologue to their own chance. Their timid and terrified appearance contrasted with the courageous audacity of the carpenter; every limb quivered with affright.

Biassou looked at them one after the other with his fox-like glance, and, as if he took a pleasure in prolonging their agony, began a discussion with Rigaud upon the different kinds of tobacco, asserting that that of Havana was only good for manufacturing cigars, whilst for snuff he knew nothing better than the Spanish tobacco, two barrels of which Bouchmaun had sent him, being a portion of the plunder of M. Lebattre's stores in the island of Tortue. Then, turning sharply upon the Citizen General C——, he asked him—

"What do you think?"

This sudden address utterly confounded the timid citizen, and he stammered out.

"General, I am entirely of your Excellency's opinion."

"You flatter me," replied Biassou; "I want *your* opinion, not mine. Do you know any tobacco that makes better snuff than that of M. Lebattres?"

"No, my lord," answered C——, whose evident terror greatly amused Biassou.

"*General, Your Excellency, My Lord!* you are an aristocrat."

"Oh no, certainly not," exclaimed the citizen general. "I am a good patriot of '91, and an ardent *negrophile*."

"Negrophile!" interrupted the general. "Pray what is a negrophile?"

"It is a friend of the blacks," stammered the citizen.

"It is not enough to be a friend of the blacks; you must also be a friend of the men of colour."

"Men of colour is what I should have said," replied the lover of the blacks, humbly. "I am mixed up with all the most famous partisans of the negroes and the mulattoes——"

Delighted at the opportunity of humiliating a white man, Biassou again interrupted him:

"*Negroes and mulattoes!* What do you mean, pray? Do you wish to insult me by making use of those terms of contempt invented by the whites? There are only men of colour and blacks here—do you understand that, Mr. Planter?"

"It was a slip, a bad habit that I picked up in childhood," answered C——. "Pardon me, my lord, I had no wish to offend you."

"Leave off this *my lording* business; I have already told you that I don't like these aristocratic ways."

C—— again endeavoured to excuse himself, and began to stammer out a fresh explanation.

"If you knew, citizen——"

"Citizen indeed!" cried Biassou, in affected anger, "I detest all this Jacobin jargon. Are you by chance a Jacobin? Remember that you are speaking to the generalissimo of the king's troops."

The unhappy partisan of the negro race was dumbfounded, and did not know in what terms to address this man who equally disdained the titles of "my lord" or "citizen," and the aristocratic or republican modes of salutation. Biassou, whose anger was only assumed, cruelly enjoyed the predicament in which he had placed him. "Alas," at last said the citizen general, "you do not do me justice, noble defender of the unwritten rights of the larger portion of the human race."

In his perplexity to hit upon an acceptable mode of address to a man who appeared to disdain all titles, he had recourse to one of those sonorous periphrases which the republicans occasionally substituted for the name and title of the persons with whom they were in conversation.

Biassou looked at him steadily and said, "You love the blacks and the men of colour?"

"Do I love them?" exclaimed the citizen C——. "Why, I correspond with Brissot and——"

Biassou interrupted him with a sardonic laugh. "Ha, ha, I am glad to find in you so trusty a friend to our cause; you must, of course, thoroughly detest those wretched colonists who punished our insurrection by a series of the most cruel executions, and you, of course, think with us, that it is not the blacks, but the whites, who are the true rebels, since they are in arms against the laws of nature and humanity? You must execrate such monsters!"

"I do execrate them," answered C——.

"Well," continued Biassou, "what do you think of a man who, in his endeavours to crush the last efforts of the slaves to regain their liberty, placed the heads of fifty black men on each side of the avenue that led to his house?"

C—— grew fearfully pale.

"What do you think of a white man who would propose to surround the town of Cap with a circle of negro heads?"

"Mercy, mercy!" cried the terrified citizen general.

"Am I threatening you?" replied Biassou, coldly. "Let me finish; a circle of heads that would reach from Fort Picolet to Cape Caracol. What do you think of that? Answer me."

The words of Biassou, "Do I threaten you," had given a faint ray of hope to C——, for he fancied that the general might have heard of this terrible proposition without knowing the author of it; he therefore replied with all the firmness that he could muster, in order to remove any impression that the idea was his own: "I consider such a suggestion an atrocious crime."

Biassou chuckled.

"Good, and what punishment should be inflicted on the man

who proposed it?"

The unfortunate C—— hesitated.

"What!" cried Biassou, "you hesitate! Are you, or are you not, the friend of the blacks?"

Of the two alternatives the wretched man chose the least threatening one, and seeing no hostile light in Biassou's eyes, he answered in a low voice—

"The guilty person deserves death."

"Well answered," replied Biassou, calmly, throwing aside the tobacco that he had been chewing.

His assumed air of indifference had completely deceived the unfortunate lover of the negro race, and he made another effort to dissipate any suspicions which might have been engendered against him.

"No one," cried he, "has a more ardent desire for your success than I. I correspond with Brissot and Pruneau de Pomme-Gouge in France, with Magaw in America, with Peter Paulus in Holland, with the Abbé Tamburini in Italy." And he was continuing to unfold the same string of names which he had formerly repeated, but with a different motive, at the council held at M. de Blanchelande's, when Biassou interrupted him.

"What do I care with whom you correspond! Tell me rather where are your granaries and store-houses, for my army has need of supplies; your plantation is doubtless a rich one, and your business must be lucrative since you correspond with so many merchants."

C—— ventured timidly to remark—

"Hero of humanity, they are not merchants, but philosophers, philanthropists, lovers of the race of blacks."

"Then," said Biassou, with a shake of his head, "if you have nothing that can be plundered, what good are you?"

This question afforded a chance of safety of which C—— eagerly availed himself.

"Illustrious warrior," exclaimed he, "have you an economist in your army?"

"What is that?" asked the general.

"It is," replied the prisoner, with as much calmness as his fears would permit him to assume, "a most necessary man, one whom all appreciate, one who follows out and classes in their proper order the respective material resources of an empire, and gives to each its real value, increasing and improving them by combining their sources and results, and pouring them like fertilizing streams into the main river of general utility, which in its turn swells the great sea of public prosperity."

"*Caramba*," observed Biassou, leaning over towards the Obi. "What the deuce does he mean by all these words strung together like the beads on your rosary?"

The Obi shrugged his shoulders in sign of ignorance and disdain as citizen C—— continued—

"If you will permit me to observe, valiant chief of the regenerators of Saint Domingo, I have carefully studied the works of the greatest economists of the world—Turgot, Raynal, and Mirabeau the friend of man. I have put their theories into practice, I thoroughly understand the science indispensable for the government of kingdoms and states———"

"The economist is not economical of his words," observed Rigaud, with his bland and cunning smile.

"But you, eternal talker," cried Biassou, "tell me, have I any kingdoms or states to govern?"

"Not yet perhaps, great man, but they will come; and besides, my knowledge descends to all the useful details which are comprised in the interior economy of an army."

The general again interrupted him: "I have nothing to do with the interior economy of the army, I command it."

"Good," replied the citizen; "you shall be the commander, I will be the commissary; I have much special knowledge as to the increase of cattle——"

"Do you think we are going to breed cattle?" cried Biassou, with his sardonic laugh. "No, my good fellow, we are content with eating them; when cattle become scarce in the French colony I shall cross the line of mountains on the frontier and take the Spanish sheep and oxen from the plains of Cotury, of La Vega, of St. Jago, and from the banks of the Yuna; if necessary I will go as far as the Island of Jamaica, and to the back of the mountain of Cibos, and from the mouths of the Neybe to those of Santo Domingo; besides, I should be glad to punish those infernal Spanish planters for giving up Ogé to the French. You see I am not uneasy as regards provisions, and so have no need of *your knowledge*."

This open declaration rather disconcerted the poor economist; he made, however, one more effort for safety. "My studies," said he, "have not been limited to the reproduction of cattle, I am acquainted with other special branches of knowledge that may be very useful to you; I can show you the method of manufacturing pitch and working coal mines."

"What do I care for that!" exclaimed Biassou. "When I want charcoal I burn a few leagues of forest."

"I can tell you the proper kinds of wood to use for shipbuilding—the *chicarm* and the *sabicca* for the keels, the *yabas* for the knees, the medlars for the framework, the *hacotnas*, the *gaïacs*, the cedars, the acomas——"

"*Que te lleven todos los demonios de los diez-y-siete infernos!*" ("May the devils of the thirty-seven hells fly away with you!"), cried Biassou, boiling over with impatience.

"I beg your pardon, my gracious patron," said the trembling economist, who did not understand Spanish.

"Listen," said Biassou, "I don't want to build vessels; there is only one vacancy that I can offer you, and that is not a very important one; I want a man to wait upon me; and now, Mr. Philosopher, tell me if that will suit you; you will have to serve me on your bended knees, you will prepare my pipe, cook my *calalou* and turtle soup, and you will stand behind me with a fan of peacock or parrot feathers like those two pages; now will the situation suit you?"

Citizen C——, whose only desire was to save his life, bent to the earth with a thousand expressions of joy and gratitude.

"You accept my offer, then?" asked Biassou.

"Can you ask such a question, generous master? do you think that I should hesitate for a moment in accepting so distinguished a post as that of being in constant attendance on you?"

At this reply the diabolical sneer of Biassou became more pronounced. He rose up with an air of triumph, crossed his arms on his chest, and thrusting aside with his foot the white man's head who was prostrate on the ground before him, he cried in a loud voice—

"I am delighted at being able to fathom how far the cowardice of the white man could go, I have already measured the extent of his cruelty. Citizen C——, it is to you that I owe this double experience. I knew all; how could you have been sufficiently besotted to think that I did not? It was you who presided at the executions of June, July, and August; it was you who placed fifty negro heads on each side of your avenue; it was you who proposed to slaughter the five hundred negroes who were confined in irons after the revolt, and to encircle the town of Cap with their heads from Fort Picolet to Cape Caracol. If you could have done it you would have placed my head amongst them, and now you think yourself lucky if I will take you as my body-servant. No, no! I have more regard for your honour than you yourself have, and I will not inflict this affront on you; prepare to die!"

At a gesture of his hand the negroes removed the unhappy lover of the blacks to a position near me, where overwhelmed by the honour of his position, he fell to the ground without being able to articulate a word.

CHAPTER XXXI.

"It is your turn now," said the general, turning to the last of the prisoners, the planter who was accused by the white men of having black blood in his veins, and who had on that account sent me a challenge.

A general clamour drowned the reply of the planter. "Muerte! Death! Mort! Touyé!" cried the negroes, grinding their teeth, and shaking their fists at the unhappy captive.

"General," said a mulatto, making himself heard above the uproar, "he is a white man, and he must die."

The miserable planter, by cries and gesticulations, managed to edge in some words. "No, general, no, my brothers, it is an infamous calumny, I am a mulatto like yourselves, of mixed blood; my mother was a negress, like your mothers and sisters."

"He lies," cried the infuriated negroes, "he is a white man, he has always detested the coloured people."

"Never," retorted the prisoner; "it is the whites that I detest; I have always said with you, '*Negre cé blan, blan cé negre*' ('The negroes are the masters, the whites are the slaves')."

"Not at all," cried the crowd, "not at all; kill the white man, kill him!"

Still the unhappy wretch kept repeating in heart-rending accents, "I am a mulatto, I am one of yourselves."

"Give me a proof," was Biassou's sole reply.

"A proof," answered the prisoner, wildly, "the proof is that the whites have always despised me."

"That may be true," returned Biassou, "but you are an insolent hound to tell us so."

A young mulatto stepped to the front and addressed the planter in an excited manner.

"That the whites despised you is a fact; but, on the other hand, you affected to look down upon the mulattoes amongst whom they classed you. It has even been reported that you once challenged a white man who called you a half caste."

A howl of execration arose from the crowd, and the cry of "death" was repeated more loudly than ever, whilst the planter, casting an appealing glance at me, continued, with tears in his eyes—

"It is a calumny, my greatest glory and happiness is in belonging to the blacks, I am a mulatto."

"If you really were a mulatto," observed Rigaud, quietly, "you would not make use of such an expression."

"How do I know what I am saying?" asked the panic-stricken wretch. "General, the proof that I am of mixed blood is in the black circle that you see round the bottom of my nails."

Biassou thrust aside the suppliant hand.

"I do not possess the knowledge of our chaplain, who can tell what a man is by looking at his hand. But listen to me: my soldiers accuse you—some, of being a white man; others, of being a false brother. If this is the case you ought to die. You, on the other hand, assert that you belong to our race, and that you have never denied it. There is one method by which you can prove your assertions. Take this dagger and stab these two white prisoners!"

As he spoke, with a wave of his hand, he designated the citizen C—— and myself.

The planter drew back from the dagger which, with a devilish smile on his face, Biassou presented to him.

"What," said the general, "do you hesitate? It is your only chance of proving your assertion to the army that you are not a white, and are one of ourselves. Come, decide at once, for we have no time to lose."

The prisoner's eyes glared wildly; he stretched out his hand towards the dagger, then let his arm fall again, turning away his head, whilst every limb quivered with emotion.

"Come, come," cried Biassou, in tones of impatience and anger, "I am in a hurry. Choose—either kill them, or die with them!"

The planter remained motionless, as if he had been turned to stone.

"Good!" said Biassou, turning towards the negroes, "he does not wish to be the executioner, let him be the victim. I can see that he is nothing but a white man—away with him!"

The negroes advanced to seize him. This movement impelled him to immediate choice between giving or receiving death.

Extreme cowardice produces a bastard species of courage.

Stepping forward, he snatched the dagger that Biassou still held out to him, and without giving himself time to reflect upon what he was about to do, he precipitated himself like a tiger upon citizen C——, who was lying on the ground near me. Then a terrible struggle commenced. The lover of the negro race, who had, at the conclusion of his interview with Biassou, remained plunged in a state of despair and stupor, had hardly noticed the scene between the general and the planter, so absorbed was he in the thought of his approaching death; but when he saw the man rush upon him, and the steel gleam above his head, the imminence of his danger aroused him at once. He started to his feet, grasped the arm of his would-be murderer, and exclaimed in a voice of terror—

"Pardon, pardon! What are you doing? What have I done?"

"You must die, sir," said the half-caste, fixing his frenzied eyes upon his victim, and endeavouring to disengage his arm. "Let me do it; I will not hurt you."

"Die by your hand," cried the economist; "but why? Spare me; you wish perhaps to kill me because I used to say that you were a mulatto. But spare my life, and I vow that I will always declare that you are a white man. Yes, you are white, I will say so everywhere, but spare me!"

The unfortunate man had taken the wrong method of sueing for mercy.

"Silence, silence!" cried the half-caste, furious at the idea of the danger he was incurring, and fearing that the negroes would hear the assertion.

But the other cried louder than ever, that he knew that he was a white man, and of good family.

The half-caste made a last effort to impose silence on him; then finding his efforts vain, he thrust aside his arms, and pressed the dagger upon C——'s breast.

The unhappy man felt the point of the weapon, and in his despair bit the arm that was driving the dagger home.

"Monster! wretch!" exclaimed he, "you are murdering me." Then casting a glance of supplication towards Biassou, he cried, "Defend me, avenger of humanity."

Then the murderer pressed more heavily on the dagger; a gush of blood bubbled over his fingers, and spattered his face. The knees of the unhappy lover of the negro race bent beneath him, his arms fell by his side, his eyes closed, he uttered a stifled groan, and fell dead.

CHAPTER XXXII.

I was paralyzed with horror at this scene, in which I every moment expected to play an important part. The *Avenger of Humanity* had gazed on the struggle without a lineament of his features changing. When all was over, he turned to his terrified pages. "More tobacco," said he, and began to chew calmly.

The Obi and Rigaud were equally impassible, but the negroes

appeared terrified at the horrible drama that their general had caused to be enacted before them.

One white man, however, yet remained to be slaughtered—my turn had come. I cast a glance upon the murderer who was about to become my executioner, and a feeling of pity came over me. His lips were violet, his teeth chattered, a convulsive tremor caused every limb to quiver. By a mechanical movement his hand was continually passed over his forehead, as if to obliterate the traces of the blood which had so liberally sprinkled it; he looked with an air of terrified wonder at the bleeding body which lay at his feet, as though he were unable to detach his strained eyeballs from the spectacle of his victim.

I waited for the moment when he would resume his task of blood. The position was a strange one: he had already tried to kill me and failed, to prove that he was white, and now he was going to murder me to show that he was black.

"Come," said Biassou, addressing him, "this is good; I am pleased with you, my friend." Then glancing at me, he added. "You need not finish the other one; and now I declare you one of us, and name you executioner to the army."

At these words a negro stepped out of the ranks, and bowing three times to the general, cried out in his jargon—which I will spare you—

"And I, general?"

"Well, what do you want?" asked Biassou.

"Are you going to do nothing for me, general?" asked the negro. "Here you give an important post to this dog of a white, who murders to save his own skin, and to prove that he is one of ourselves. Have you no post to give to me, who am a true black?"

This unexpected request seemed to embarrass Biassou, and Rigaud whispered to him in French—

"You can't satisfy him; try to elude his request."

"You wish for promotion, then?" asked Biassou of the *true black*. "Well, I am willing enough to grant it to you. What grade do you wish for?"

"I wish to be an officer."

"An officer, eh?—and what are your claims to the epaulet founded on?"

"It was I," answered the negro, emphatically, "who set fire to the house of Lagoscelte in the first days of August last. It was I who murdered M. Clement the planter, and carried the head of his sugar refiner on my pike. I killed ten white women and seven small children, one of whom on the point of a spear served as a standard for Bouckmann's brave blacks. Later on I burnt alive the families of four colonists, whom I had locked up in the strong room of Fort Galifet. My father was broken on the wheel at Cap, my brother was hung at Rocrow, and I narrowly escaped being shot. I have burnt three coffee plantations, six indigo estates, and two hundred acres of sugar-cane; I murdered my master, M. Noé, and his mother——"

"Spare us the recital of your services," said Rigaud, whose feigned benevolence was the mask for real cruelty, but who was ferocious with decency, and could not listen to this cynical confession of deeds of violence.

"I could quote many others," continued the negro, proudly, "but you will no doubt consider that these are sufficient to insure my promotion, and to entitle me to wear a gold epaulet like my comrades there," pointing to the staff of Biassou.

The general affected to reflect for a few minutes, and then

gravely addressed the negro.

"I am satisfied with your services, and should be pleased to promote you, but you must satisfy me on one point. Do you understand Latin?"

The astonished negro opened his eyes widely.

"Eh, general?" said he.

"Yes," repeated Biassou, quickly; "do you understand Latin?"

"La—Latin?" stammered the astonished negro.

"Yes, yes, yes, Latin; do you understand Latin?" said the cunning chief, and unfolding a banner upon which was embroidered the verse from the Psalms, "*In exitu Israël de Egypto*," he added, "Explain the meaning of these words."

The negro, in complete ignorance of what was meant, remained silent and motionless, fumbling with the waistband of his trousers, whilst his astonished eyes wandered from the banner to the general, and from the general back again to the banner.

"Come, go on," exclaimed Biassou, impatiently.

The negro opened and shut his mouth several times, scratched his head, and at last said slowly—

"I don't understand it, general."

"How, scoundrel!" cried Biassou; "you wish to become an officer, and you do not understand Latin!"

"But, general," stammered the puzzled negro.

"Silence," roared Biassou, whose anger appeared to increase; "I do not know what prevents me from having you shot at once. Did you ever hear such a thing, Rigaud? he wants to be an officer, and does not understand Latin. Well then, idiot, as you do not understand, I will explain what is written on this banner: *In exitu*—every soldier, *Israël*—who does not understand Latin, *de Egypto*—cannot be made an officer. Is not that the translation, reverend sir?"

The Obi bowed his head in the affirmative, and Biassou continued—

"This brother of whom you are jealous, and whom I have appointed executioner, understands Latin!"

He turned to the new executioner—

"You know Latin, do you not? prove it to this blockhead. What is the meaning of *Dominus vobiscum*?"

The unhappy half-caste, roused from his gloomy reverie by the dreaded voice, raised his head, and though his brain was still troubled by the cowardly murder that he had just committed, terror compelled him to be obedient.

There was something pitiable in his manner, as his mind went back to his schooldays, and in the midst of his terrible feelings and remorse he repeated, in the tone of a child saying its lesson, "*Dominus vobiscum*—that means, 'May the Lord be with you.'"

"*Et cum spirito tuo*," added the mysterious Obi, solemnly.

"Amen," repeated Biassou; then resuming his angry manner, and mingling with his reproaches some Latin phrases to impress the negroes with the superior attainments of their chief, he cried, "Go to the rear rank, *sursum corda*; never attempt to enter the places of those who know Latin, *orate fratres*, or I will have you hung. *Bonus, bona, bonum!*"

The astonished and terrified negro slunk away, greeted by the hoots and hisses of his comrades, who were indignant at his presumption, and impressed with the deep learning of their general.

Burlesque though this scene was, it inspired me with a very

high idea of Biassou's administrative capabilities. He had made ridicule the means of repressing ambitious aspirations, which are always so dangerous to authority in undisciplined bodies; and his cunning gave me a fuller idea of his mental powers, and the crass ignorance of the negroes under his command.

CHAPTER XXXIII.

The breakfast hour had now arrived; the shell of a turtle was placed before Biassou, in which smoked a species of *olla-podrida* seasoned with bacon, in which turtle flesh took the place of lamb; an enormous carib cabbage floated on the surface of the stew, and in addition, on strips of bark, were dried raisins and water-melons, a loaf of maize bread; and a bottle of wine, bound round with tarred string, completed the feast. Biassou took from his pocket a few heads of garlic and rubbed his bread with them; then, without even ordering the bleeding form to be carried away, he began to eat, inviting Rigaud to do the same.

There was something terrible in Biassou's appetite.

The Obi did not join their repast; like others in his profession, I could easily understand that he never took anything in public, to induce a belief amongst the negroes that he lived entirely without food.

During breakfast, Biassou ordered one of his aides-de-camp to order the march past to commence, and the different corps began to defile past in fairly good order. The negroes of Morne-Rouge were the first; there were about four thousand of them, divided into companies commanded by chiefs, who were distinguished by their scarlet breeches and sashes. This force was composed of tall and powerful negroes; some of them carried guns, axes, and sabres, but many had no other arms than bows and arrows, and javelins rudely fashioned by themselves. They carried no standard, and moved past in mournful silence. As they marched on, Biassou whispered to Rigaud—

"When will Blanchelande's and Rouvray's shot and shell free me from these bandits of Morne-Rouge? I hate them, they are nearly all of them *Congos*, and they only believe in killing in open battle—following the example of their chief Bug-Jargal, a young fool, who plays at being generous and magnanimous. You do not know him, Rigaud, and I hope you never will, for the whites have taken him prisoner, and they may perhaps rid me of him, as they did of Bouckmann."

"Speaking of Bouckmann," answered Rigaud, "there are the negroes of Macaya just passing, and I see in their ranks the negro whom Jean François sent to you with the news of Bouckmann's death. Do you know that that man might upset all the prophecies of the Obi, if he were to say that he had been kept for more than half an hour at the outposts, and that he had told me the news before you sent for him?"

"Diabolo!" answered Biassou, "you are in the right, my friend; this man's mouth must be shut. Wait a bit."

Then raising his voice he called out "Macaya." The leader of the division left the ranks, and approached the general with the stock of his firelock reversed, in token of respect.

"Make that man who does not belong to your division leave his rank and come forward."

Macaya speedily brought the messenger of Jean François before the general, who at once assumed that appearance of anger which he knew so well how to simulate.

"Who are you?" cried he.

"General, I am a black."

"Carramba, I can see that well enough; but what is your name?"

"My name is Vavelan, my patron saint is Sabas, deacon and martyr, whose feast is on the twentieth day before the Nativity of our Lord."

Biassou interrupted him.

"How dare you present yourself on parade, amidst shining muskets and white cross-belts, with your sword without a sheath, your breeches torn, and your feet muddy?"

"General," answered the negro, "it is not my fault. I was despatched by the Grand Admiral, Jean François, to bring you the news of the death of the chief of the English negroes; and if my clothes are torn and my feet bemired, it is because I have run, without stopping to take breath, to bring you the news as soon as possible, but they detained me at——"

Biassou frowned.

"I did not ask you about that, but how you dared to enter the ranks in so unbecoming a dress. Commend your soul to Saint Sabas, your patron, the deacon and martyr, and go and get yourself shot."

And here I had another proof of the ascendency that Biassou exercised over the insurgents. The unfortunate man who was ordered to go and get himself executed did not utter a protest; he bowed his head, crossed his arms on his breast, saluted his pitiless judge three times, and after having knelt to the Obi, who gave him plenary absolution, he left the cavern.

A few minutes afterwards a volley of musketry told us that Biassou's commands had been obeyed, and that the negro was no more.

Freed from all sources of uneasiness, the general turned to Rigaud, a gleam of pleasure in his eye, and gave a triumphant chuckle which seemed to say—"Admire me!"

CHAPTER XXXIV.

But the march past still continued. This army, which had presented so curious a spectacle in camp, had a no less extraordinary appearance under arms. Sometimes a horde of almost naked negroes would come along armed with clubs and tomahawks, marching to the notes of a goat's horn like mere savages; then would come regiments of mulattoes, dressed in the English or Spanish manner, well armed and equipped, regulating the pace by the roll of the drum; then a band of negresses and their children carrying forks and spits, then some tag-rag bent under the weight of an old musket without lock or barrel; *griotes* with their feathered aprons, *griots* dancing with hideous contortions, and singing incoherent airs to the accompaniment of guitars, tom-toms, and balafos. Then would be a procession of priests, or Obi men, half-castes, quarter-castes, free mulattoes, or wandering hordes of escaped slaves with a proud look of liberty on their faces and shining muskets on their shoulders, dragging in their ranks well-filled waggons, or some artillery taken from the whites, which were looked on more as trophies than as military engines, and yelling out at the top of their voices the songs of Grand-Pré and Oua-Nassé. Above their heads floated flags, banners, and standards of every form, colour, and device—white, red, tricolour, with the lilies, with the cap of liberty, bearing inscriptions—*Death to Priests and Nobles*; *Long live Religion*; *Liberty and Equality*; *Long live the King*; *Viva España*; *No more Tyrants*, &c.;—a confusion of sentiments which showed that the insurgents were a mere crowd collected together, with ideas as different as were the men who composed it. On passing in their turn before the cave the companies drooped their banners, and Biassou returned the salute. He addressed every band either in praise or censure, and each word that dropped from his mouth was received by his men with fanatical respect or superstitious dread.

The wave of savage soldiery passed away at last. I confess that the sight that had at first afforded some distraction to my feelings, finished by wearying me. The sun went down as the last ranks filed away, and his last rays cast a copper-coloured hue upon the granite portals of the cave.

CHAPTER XXXV.

Biassou seemed to be dreaming. When the review was concluded, his last orders had been given, and the insurgents had retired to the huts, he condescended to address me again.

"Young man," said he, "you have now had the means of

judging of my power and genius; the time has now arrived for you to bear the report to Leogri."

"It is not my fault that he has not had it earlier," answered I, coldly.

"You are right," replied Biassou. He then paused, as if to note what the effect would be upon me of what he was going to say, and then added, "But it will depend upon yourself whether you ever carry the message or not."

"What do you mean?" exclaimed I, in astonishment.

"Why," replied he, "that your life depends upon yourself, and that you can save it if you will."

This sudden paroxysm of pity—the first, and no doubt the last, which had ever possessed Biassou—surprised me much, and astonished the Obi so greatly that he leapt from the position which he had so long maintained, and, placing himself face to face with the general, addressed him in angry tones.

"What are you saying? Have you forgotten your promise? Neither God nor you can dispose of this life, for it belongs to me."

At that instant I thought that I recognized the voice; but it was but a fleeting recollection, and in a moment had passed away.

Biassou got up from his seat without betraying any anger, spoke for a few moments in whispers to the Obi, and pointed to the black flag which I had already remarked, and after a little more conversation the Obi nodded in sign of assent. Both of them then reverted to their former positions.

"Listen to me," said the general, drawing from his pocket the dispatch which Jean François had sent to him. "Things are going ill. Bouckmann has been killed. The whites have slaughtered more than two thousand of our men in the district of Cul-de-Sac. The colonists are continuing to establish and to fortify military posts. By our own folly we have lost the chance of taking Cap, and it will be long before another occasion will present itself. On the eastern side our line of march has been cut by a river, and the whites have defended the passage by a pontoon battery and a fortified camp. On the south side they have planted artillery on the mountainous road called the Haut-du-Cap. The position is, in addition, defended by a strong stockade, at which all the inhabitants have laboured, and in front of it there is a strong *chevaux de frise*. Cap, therefore, is beyond our reach. Our ambush in the ravines of Dompté-Mulâtre was a failure; and, to add to all these misfortunes, the Siamese fever has devastated our camps. In consequence, the Grand Admiral (and I agree with him) has decided to treat with the Governor Blanchelande and the Colonial Assembly. Here is the letter that we have addressed to the assembly on this matter. Listen!

" 'Gentlemen of the House of Deputies,—

" 'In the great misfortunes which have afflicted this great and important colony we have also been enveloped, and there remains nothing for us to say in justification of our conduct. One day you will render us the justice that our conduct merits.

" 'According to us, the King of Spain is a good king who treats us well, and has *testified it to us by rewards*; so we shall continue to serve him with zeal and devotion.

" 'We see by the law of September 28, 1791, that the National Assembly and the King have agreed to settle definitely the status of slaves, and the political situation of people of colour. We will defend the decrees of the National Assembly with the last drop of our blood.

" 'It would be most interesting to us if you would declare, by an order sanctioned by your general, as to your intentions regarding the position of the slaves. Knowing that they are the objects of your solicitude through their chiefs, who send you this, they will be satisfied if the relations now broken are once again resumed.

" 'Do not count, gentlemen Deputies, upon our consenting to take up arms for the revolutionary Assemblies. We are the subjects of three kings—the King of Congo, the born master of all the blacks; the King of France, who represents our fathers; and the King of Spain, who is the representative of our mothers. These three kings are the descendants of those who, conducted by a star, worshipped the Man God. If we were to consent to serve the Assemblies, we might be forced to take up arms and to make war against our brothers, the subjects of those three kings to whom we have sworn fidelity. And, besides, we do not know what is meant by the will of the Nation, seeing that since the world has been in existence we have always executed that of the King. The Prince of France loves us; the King of Spain never ceases to help us. We aid them—they aid us; it is the cause of humanity; and, besides, if these kings should fail us we could soon *enthrone a king of our own.*

" 'Such are our intentions, although we now consent to make peace.

" '*Signed*, Jean François, General; Biassou, Brigadier; Desprez, Manzeau, Toussaint, Aubert, Commissaires; *ad hoc.*' "[3]

"You see," said Biassou, after he had read this piece of negro diplomacy, every word of which has remained imprinted on my memory, "that our intentions are peaceable; but this is what we want you to do: neither Jean François nor I have been brought up in the schools of the whites, or learned the niceties of their language. We know how to fight, but not how to write. Now we do not wish that there should be anything in our letter at which our former masters could laugh. You seem to have learned those frivolous accomplishments in which we are lacking. Correct any faults you may find in this dispatch, so that it may excite no derision amongst the whites, and—I will give you your life!"

This proposition of becoming the corrector of Biassou's faults of spelling and composition was too repugnant to my pride for me to hesitate for a moment; and besides, what did I care for life. I declined his offer. He appeared surprised.

"What!" exclaimed he, "you prefer death to scrawling a few marks with a pen on a piece of paper?"

"Yes," replied I.

My determination seemed to embarrass him. After a few moments of thought he again addressed me.

"Listen, young fool. I am less obstinate than you are; I give you until to-morrow evening, up to the setting of the sun, when you shall again be brought before me. Think well then, before you refuse to obey my wishes. Adieu. Let night bring reflection to you, and remember that with us death is not simply death—much comes before you reach it."

The frightful sardonic grin with which he concluded his last speech too plainly brought to my recollection the awful tortures which it was Biassou's greatest pleasure to inflict upon his prisoners.

"Candi," continued Biassou, "remove the prisoner, and give him in charge to the men of Morne-Rouge. I wish him to live for another day, and perhaps my other soldiers would not have the patience to let him do so." The mulatto Candi, who commanded the guard, caused my arms to be bound behind my back, a soldier took hold of the end of the cord, and we left the grotto.

[3] It is a fact that this ridiculously characteristic letter was sent to the Assembly.

CHAPTER XXXVI.

When any extraordinary events, unexpected anxieties or catastrophes, intrude themselves suddenly into a life up to that period peaceful and happy, these unexpected emotions interrupt the repose of the soul which lay dreaming in the monotony of prosperity. Misfortune which comes on you in this manner does not seem like an awakening from bliss, but rather like a dream of evil. With the man who has been invariably happy, despair begins with stupor. Unexpected misery is like cramp—it clasps, and deadens everything. Men, acts, and things, at that time pass before us like a fantastic apparition, and move along as if in a dream. Everything in the horizon of our life is changed, both the atmosphere and the perspective, but it still goes on for a long time before our eyes have lost that sort of luminous image of past happiness which follows in its train, and interposes without cessation between it and the sombre present. Then everything that is, appears to be unreal and ridiculous, and we can scarcely believe in our own existence, because we find nothing around us that formerly used to compose our life, and we cannot understand how all can have gone away without taking us with it, and why nothing of our life remains to us.

Were this strained position of the soul to continue long, it would disturb the equilibrium of the brain and become madness—a state happier perhaps than that which remains, for life then is nothing but a vision of past misfortune, acting like a ghost.

CHAPTER XXXVII.

Gentlemen, I hardly know why I lay before you my ideas upon such a subject; they are not those which you understand, or can be made to understand. To thoroughly comprehend them, you must have gone through what I have. But such was the state of my mind when the guards of Biassou handed me over to the negroes of Morne-Rouge. I was still in a dream: it appeared as if one body of phantoms passed me over to another, and without opposing any resistance I permitted them to bind me by the middle to a tree. They then gave me some boiled potatoes, which I ate with the mechanical instinct that God grants to man even in the midst of overwhelming thought.

The darkness had now come on, and my guards took refuge in their huts, with the exception of half a dozen who remained with me, lying before a large fire that they had lighted to preserve themselves from the cold night-air. In a few moments they were all buried in profound sleep.

The state of physical weakness into which I had fallen caused my thoughts to wander in a strange manner. I thought of those calm and peaceful days which, but a few weeks ago, I had passed with Marie, without being able to foresee any future but one of continued happiness. I compared them with the day that had just expired, a day in which so many strange events had occurred as almost to make me wonder whether I was not labouring under some delusion. I had been three times condemned to death, and still remained under sentence. I thought of my future, bounded only by the morrow, and which offered nothing but misfortune, and a death happily near at hand. I seemed to be the victim of some terrible nightmare. Again and again I asked myself if all that had happened was real: was I really in the power of the sanguinary Biassou, and was my Marie lost to me for ever? Could this prisoner, guarded by six savages, bound to a tree, and condemned to certain death, really be me? In spite of all my efforts to repel them, the thoughts of Marie would force themselves upon me. In anguish I thought of her fate, I strained my bonds in my efforts to break them, and to fly to her succour, ever hoping that the terrible dream would pass away; and that Heaven would not permit all the horrors that I dreaded to fall upon the head of her, who had been united to me in a sacred bond. In my sad preoccupation the thought of Pierrot returned to me, and rage nearly took away my senses; the pulses of my temples throbbed nearly to bursting. I hated him, I cursed him; I despised myself for having ever had friendship for Pierrot at the same time I had felt love for Marie; and without caring to seek for the motive which had urged him to cast himself into the waters of Grande-Riviere, I wept because he had escaped me. He was dead, and I was about to die, and all that I regretted was that I had been unable to wreak my vengeance upon him.

During the state of semi-somnolency into which my weakness had plunged me, these thoughts passed through my brain. I do not know how long it lasted, but I was aroused by a man's voice singing distinctly, but at some distance, the old Spanish song, "*Yo que soy contrabandista.*" Quivering with emotion I opened my eyes; all was dark around me, the negroes slept, the fire was dying down. I could hear nothing more. I fancied that the voice must have been a dream, and my sleep-laden eyelids closed again. In a second I opened them; again I heard the voice singing sadly but much nearer, the same song—

'Twas on the field of Ocanen
   That I fell in their power,
To Cotadilla taken,
   Unhappy from that hour.

This time it was not a charm—it *was* Pierrot's voice. A few moments elapsed, then it rose again through the silence and the gloom, and once more I heard the well-known air of "*Yo soy que contrabandista.*" A dog ran eagerly to greet me, and rolled at my feet in token of welcome; it was Rask! A tall negro stood facing me, and the glimmer of the fire threw his shadow, swelled to colossal proportions, upon the sward; it was Pierrot!

The thirst for vengeance fired my brain; surprise rendered me motionless and dumb. I was not asleep. Could the dead return? If not a dream, it must be an apparition. I turned from him with horror.

When he saw me do this, his head sank upon his breast.

"Brother," murmured he, "you promised that you would never doubt me when you heard me sing that song. My brother, have you forgotten your promise?"

Rage restored the power of speech to me.

"Monster," exclaimed I, "do I see you at last! Butcher, murderer of my uncle, ravisher of Marie, dare you call me your brother? Do not venture to approach me."

I forgot that I was too securely tied to make the slightest movement, and glanced to my left side as though to seek my sword.

My intention did not escape him, and he continued in a sorrowful tone of voice—

"No, I will not come near you—you are unhappy and I pity you; whilst you have no pity for me, though I am much more wretched than you are."

I shrugged my shoulders; he understood my feelings, and in a half dreamy manner continued—

"Yes, you have lost much; but, believe me, I have lost more than you have."

But the sound of our conversation had aroused the negro guard. Perceiving a stranger they leapt to their feet, and seized their weapons; but as soon as they recognized the intruder they uttered a cry of surprise and joy, and cast themselves at his feet, striking the ground with their foreheads.

But the homage that the negroes rendered to Pierrot, and the fondlings of Rask, made no impression upon me at the moment. I was boiling over with passion, and maddened at the bonds that restrained me, and at length my fury found words. "Oh, how unhappy I am!" I exclaimed, shedding tears of rage. "I was grieving because I thought that this wretch had committed suicide, and robbed me of my just revenge; and now he is here to mock me, living and breathing under my very eyes, and I am powerless to stab him to the heart. Is there no one to free me from these accursed cords?"

Pierrot turned to the negroes, who where still prostrate before him.

"Comrades," said he, "release the prisoner."

CHAPTER XXXVIII.

He was promptly obeyed. With the greatest eagerness my guards cut asunder the ropes that confined me. I rose up free, but I remained motionless, for surprise rooted me to the spot.

"That is not all," said Pierrot, and snatching a dagger from one of the negroes, he handed it to me. "You can now have your wish; Heaven would not be pleased should I dispute your right to dispose of my life. Three times you have preserved it. Strike, it is yours, I say, and if you wish, strike!"

There was no sign of anger or of bitterness in his face; he appeared resigned and mournful.

The very vengeance offered to me by the man with whom I had so much longed to stand face to face, prevented my seizing the opportunity. I felt that all my hatred for Pierrot, all my love for Marie, could not induce me to commit a cowardly murder; besides, however damning appearances might be, yet a voice from the depths of my heart warned me that no criminal, no guilty man, would thus dare to stand before me and brave my vengeance. Shall I confess it to you, there was a certain imperious fascination about this extraordinary being which conquered me in spite of myself; I pushed aside the dagger he offered to me.

"Wretch," cried I, "I wish to kill you in fair fight, but I am no assassin. Defend yourself."

"Defend myself," replied he, in tones of astonishment, "and against whom?"

"Against me!"

He started back. "Against you! that is the only thing in which I cannot obey you. Look at Rask there—I could easily kill him, for he would let me do it; but as for making him fight me, the thing would be impossible, he would not understand me if I told him to do so. I do not understand you; in your case I am Rask."

After a short silence, he added, "I see the gleam of hate in your eyes, as you once saw it in mine. I know that you have suffered much, that your uncle has been murdered, your plantations burned, your friends slaughtered—yes, they have plundered your house, and devastated your inheritance; but it was not I that did these things, it was my people. Listen to me. I one day told you that your people had done me much injury, you said that you must not be blamed for the acts of others. What was my reply?"

His face grew brighter as he awaited my reply, evidently expecting that I should embrace him; but fixing an angry gaze upon him, I answered—

"You disdain all responsibility as to the acts of your people, but you say nothing about what you have yourself done."

"What have I done?" asked he.

I stepped up close to him, and in a voice of thunder I demanded, "Where is Marie? what have you done with Marie?"

At this question a cloud passed over his face; he seemed momentarily embarrassed. At last he spoke. "Maria!" said he, "yes; you are right—but too many ears listen to us here."

His embarrassment, the words "You are right," raised the hell of jealousy in my heart, yet still he gazed upon me with a perfectly open countenance, and in a voice trembling with emotion said, "Do not suspect me, I implore you. Besides, I will tell you everything; love me, as I love you, with perfect trust."

He paused to mark the effect of his words, and then added tenderly, "May I not again call you brother?"

But I was a prey to my jealous feelings, and his friendly words seemed to me but the deep machinations of a hypocrite, and only served to exasperate me more. "Dare you recall the time when you did so, you monster of ingratitude?" I exclaimed.

He interrupted me, a tear shining in his eye: "It is not I who am ungrateful."

"Well then," I continued, "tell me what you have done with Marie?"

"Not here, not here," answered he, "other ears than ours listen to our words; besides, you would not believe me, and time presses. The day has come, and you must be removed from this. All is at an end. Since you doubt me, far better would it have been for you to take the dagger and finish all; but wait a little before you take what you call your vengeance—I must first free you. Come with me to Biassou."

His manner, both in speaking and acting, concealed a mystery which I could not understand. In spite of all my prejudices against the man, his voice always made my heart vibrate. In listening to him a certain hidden power that he possessed subjugated me. I found myself hesitating between vengeance and pity, between the bitterest distrust and the blindest confidence. I followed him.

CHAPTER XXXIX.

We left the camp of the negroes of Morne-Rouge. I could not help thinking it strange to find myself at perfect liberty amongst a horde of savages, in a spot where the evening before each man had seemed only too ready to shed my blood. Far from seeking to bar our progress, both the negroes and the mulattoes prostrated themselves on all sides, with exclamations of surprise, joy, and respect. I was ignorant what rank Pierrot held in the army of the insurgents, but I remembered the influence that he used to exercise over his companions in slavery, and this appeared to me to account for the respect with which he was now treated.

On our arrival at the guard before the grotto, the mulatto Candi advanced before us with threatening gestures, demanding how we dared approach so near the general's quarters; but when he came near enough to recognize my conductor, he hurriedly removed his gold-laced cap, as though terrified at his own audacity, bowed to the ground, and at once introduced us into Biassou's presence, with a thousand apologies of which Pierrot took no heed.

The respect with which the simple negro soldiers had treated

Pierrot excited my surprise very little, but seeing Candi, one of the principal officers of the army, humiliate himself thus before my uncle's slave, made me ask myself who this man could be whose power was illimitable. How much more astonished was I, then, upon being introduced into the presence of Biassou, who was alone when we entered, and was quietly enjoying his *calalou*. He started to his feet, concealing disappointment and surprise under the appearance of profound respect, bowed humbly to my companion, and offered him his mahogany throne.

Pierrot declined it. "No, Jean Biassou," said he, "I have not come to take your place, but simply to ask a favour at your hands."

"Your Highness," answered Biassou, redoubling his obeisances, "you know well that all Jean Biassou has is yours, and that you can dispose as freely of all as you can of Jean Biassou himself."

"I do not ask for so much," replied Pierrot, quickly; "all I ask is the life and liberty of this prisoner," and he pointed to me.

For a moment Biassou appeared embarrassed, but he speedily recovered himself.

"Your servant is in despair, your Highness, for you ask of him, to his great regret, more than he can grant; he is not Jean Biassou's prisoner, does not belong to Jean Biassou, and has nothing to do with Jean Biassou."

"What do you mean?" asked Pierrot, in severe tones, "by saying that he does not belong to you? Does any one else hold authority here except you?"

"Alas, yes, your Highness."

"Who is it?"

"My army."

The sly and obsequious manner in which Biassou eluded the frank and haughty questions of Pierrot, showed, had it depended solely upon himself, he would gladly have treated his visitor with far less respect than he felt himself now compelled to do.

"What!" exclaimed Pierrot, "your army; and do not you command it?"

Biassou, with every appearance of sincerity, replied—

"Does your Highness really think that we can command men who are in insurrection because they will not obey?"

I cared too little for my life to break the silence that I had imposed upon myself, else, having seen the day before the despotic authority that Biassou exercised over his men, I could have contradicted his assertions, and laid bare his duplicity to Pierrot.

"Well, if you have no authority over your men, and if they are your masters, what reason can they have for hating your prisoner?"

"Bouckmann has been killed by the white troops," answered Biassou, endeavouring to conceal his sardonic smile under a mask of sorrow, "and my men are determined to avenge upon this white the death of the chief of the Jamaica negroes. They wish to show trophy against trophy, and desire that the head of this young officer should serve as a counterpoise to the head of Bouckmann in the scales in which the good *Giu* weighs both parties."

"Do you still continue to carry on this horrible system of reprisals. Listen to me, Jean Biassou: it is these cruelties that are the ruin of our just cause. Prisoner as I was in the camp of the whites (from which I have managed to escape), I had not heard of the death of Bouckmann until you told me. It is the just punishment of heaven for his crimes. I will tell you another piece of news: Jeannot, the negro chief who served as a guide to draw the white troops into the ambush of Dompté-Mulâtre, Jeannot also is dead. You know—do not interrupt me, Biassou—that he rivalled you and Bouckmann in his atrocities; and pay attention to this, it was not the thunderbolt of heaven, nor the bullets of the whites, that struck him—it was Jean François himself who ordered this act of justice to be performed."

Biassou, who had listened with an air of gloomy respect, uttered an exclamation of surprise. At this moment Rigaud entered, bowed respectfully to Pierrot, and whispered in Biassou's ear.

The murmur of many voices was heard in the camp.

"Yes," continued Pierrot, "Jean François, who has no fault except a preposterous love of luxury and show, whose carriage with its six horses takes him every day to hear mass at the Grande-Riviere, Jean François himself has put a stop to the crimes of Jeannot. In spite of the cowardly entreaties of the brigand, who clung in despair to the knees of the Priest of Marmalade, who attended him in his last moments, he was shot beneath the very tree upon which he used to hang his living victims upon iron hooks. Think upon this, Biassou. Why these massacres which provoke the whites to reprisals? Why all these juggleries which only tend to excite the passions of our unhappy comrades, already too much exasperated? There is at Trou-Coffi a mulatto impostor, called Romaine the Prophet, who is in command of a fanatical band of negroes; he profanes the holy sacrament of the mass, he pretends that he is in direct communication with the Virgin, and he urges on his men to murder and pillage in the name of Marie."

There was a more tender inflection in the voice of Pierrot as he uttered this name than even religious respect would have warranted, and I felt annoyed and irritated at it.

"And you," continued he, "you have in your camp some Obi, I hear—some impostor like this Romaine the Prophet. I well know that having to lead an army composed of so many heterogeneous materials, a common bond is necessary; but can it be found nowhere save in ferocious fanaticism and ridiculous superstition? Believe me, Biassou, the white men are not so cruel as we are. I have seen many planters protect the lives of their slaves. I am not ignorant that in some cases it was not the life of a man, but a sum of money that they desired to save, but at any rate their interest gave them the appearance of a virtue. Do not let us be less merciful than they are, for it is our interest to be so. Will our cause be more holy and more just because we exterminate the women, slaughter the children, and burn the colonists in their own houses? These, however, are every-day occurrences. Answer me, Biassou: must the traces of our progress be always marked by a line of blood and fire?"

He ceased; the fire of his glance, the accent of his voice, gave to his words a force of conviction and authority which it is impossible for me to imitate. Like a fox in the clutches of a lion, Biassou seemed to seek for some means of escape from the power that constrained him. Whilst he vainly sought for a pretext, the chief of the negroes of Cayer, Rigaud, who the evening before had calmly watched the horrors that had been perpetrated in his presence, seemed to be shocked at the picture that Pierrot had drawn, and exclaimed with a hypocritical affectation of grief—

"Great heavens! how terrible is a nation when roused to fury."

CHAPTER XL.

The confusion in the camp appeared to increase, to the great uneasiness of Biassou. I heard afterwards that it was caused by the negroes of Morne-Rouge, who hurried from one end of the camp to the other, announcing the return of my liberator, and declaring their intention of supporting him in whatever object he had come to Biassou's camp for. Rigaud had informed the generalissimo of this, and it was the fear of a fatal division in the camp that prompted Biassou to make some sort of concession to the wishes of Pierrot.

"Your Highness," remarked he, with an air of injured innocence, "if we are hard on the whites, you are equally severe upon us. You are wrong in accusing us of being the cause of the torrent, for it is the torrent that drags us away with it; but *que podria hacer a hora* ("but what can I do at present") that will please you?"

"I have already told you, Señor Biassou," answered Pierrot; "let me take this prisoner away with me."

Biassou remained for a few moments silent, as though in deep thought; then putting on an expression of as great frankness as he was able, he answered—

"Your Highness, I wish to prove to you that I have every wish to please you. Permit me to have two words in private with the prisoner, and he shall be free to follow you."

"If that is all you ask, I agree," replied Pierrot.

His eyes, which up to that moment had wandered about in a distrustful manner, glistened with delight, and he moved away a few paces to leave us to our conversation.

Biassou drew me on one side into a retired part of the cavern, and said in a low voice—

"I can only spare your life upon the condition that I proposed; are you ready to fulfil it?"

He showed me the dispatch of Jean François; to consent appeared to me too humiliating.

"Never," answered I, firmly.

"Aha," repeated he, with his sardonic chuckle, "are you always as firm? You have great confidence, then, in your protector. Do you know who he is?"

"I do," answered I, quickly, "he is a monster, as you are, only he is a greater hypocrite."

He started back in astonishment, seeking to read in my glance if I spoke seriously.

"What!" exclaimed he, "do you not know him then?"

With a disdainful look, I replied—

"I only know him as my uncle's slave, and his name is Pierrot."

Again Biassou smiled bitterly.

"Aha, that indeed is strange; he asks for your life and liberty, and you say that you only know him for a monster like myself."

"What matters that?" I answered; "if I do gain a little liberty, it is not to save my own life, but to take his."

"What is that you are saying?" asked Biassou. "And yet you seem to speak as you believe; I cannot think that you would trifle with your life. There is something beneath all this that I do not understand. You are protected by a man that you hate; he insists upon your life being spared, and you, are longing to take his. But it matters little to me; you desire a short spell of freedom—it is all that I can give you. I will leave you free to follow him, but swear to me by your honour, that you will return to me and reconstitute yourself my prisoner two hours before the sun sets. You are a Frenchman, and I will trust you."

What shall I say, gentlemen. Life was a burden to me, and I hated the idea of owing it to Pierrot, for every circumstance pointed him out as a just object of my hatred. I do not think for a moment that Biassou (who did not easily permit his prey to escape him) would allow me to go free except upon his own conditions. All I desired was a few hours' liberty which I could devote to discovering the fate of my beloved before my death. Biassou, relying upon my honour as a Frenchman, would grant me these, and without hesitation I pledged it.

"Your Highness," said Biassou, in obsequious tones, "the white prisoner is at your disposal; you can take him with you, for he is free to accompany you wherever you wish."

"Thanks, Biassou," cried Pierrot, extending his hand. "You have rendered me a service which places me entirely at your disposal. Remain in command of our brethren of Morne-Rouge until my return."

Then he turned towards me—I never saw so much happiness in his eyes before.

"Since you are free," cried he, "come with me." And with a strange earnestness he drew me away with him.

Biassou looked after us with blank astonishment, which was even perceptible through the respectful leave that he took of my companion.

CHAPTER XLI.

I was longing to be alone with Pierrot. His embarrassment when I had questioned him as to the fate of Marie, the ill-concealed tenderness with which he had dared to pronounce her name, had made those feelings of hatred and jealousy which had sprung up in my heart take far deeper root than at the time I saw him bearing away through the flames of Fort Galifet, her whom I could scarcely call my wife.

What did I care for the generous indignation with which he had reproved the cruelties of Biassou, the trouble which he had taken to preserve my life, and the curious manner which marked all his words and actions. What cared I for the mystery that appeared to envelop him, which brought him living before my eyes, when I thought to have witnessed his death. He proved to be a prisoner of the white troops when I believed that he lay buried in the depths of Grande-Riviere—the slave become a king, the prisoner a liberator. Of all these incomprehensible things one was clear—Marie had been carried off by him; and I had this crime to punish, this outrage to avenge.

However strange were the events that had passed under my eyes, they were not sufficient to shake my determination, and I had waited with impatience for the moment when I could compel my rival to explain all. That moment had at last arrived.

We had passed through crowds of negroes, who cast

themselves on the ground as we pursued our way, exclaiming in tones of surprise, "*Miraculo! ya no esta prisonero!*" ("A miracle! he is no longer a prisoner!"), but whether they referred to Pierrot or to myself I neither knew nor cared. We had gained the outskirts of the camp, and rocks and trees concealed from our view the outposts of Biassou; Rask in high good humour was running in front of us, and Pierrot was following him with rapid strides, when I stopped him.

"Listen to me," cried I; "it is useless to go any farther—the ears that you dreaded can no longer listen to us. What have you done with Marie? tell me!"

Concentrated emotion made my voice tremble. He gazed upon me kindly.

"Always the same question!" said he.

"Yes, always," returned I, furiously; "always. I will put that question to you as you draw your last breath, or as I utter my last sigh. Where is Marie?"

"Can nothing, then, drive away your doubts of my loyalty? But you shall know all soon."

"Soon, monster!" repeated I, "soon; it is now, at this instant, that I want to know all. Where is Marie? where is Marie? Answer, or stake your life against mine. Defend yourself."

"I have already told you," answered he, sadly, "that that is impossible; the stream will not struggle against its source, and my life, which you have three times saved, cannot contend against yours. Besides, even if I wished it the thing is impossible; we have but one dagger between us."

As he spoke, he drew the weapon from his girdle and offered it to me.

"Take it," said he.

I was beside myself with passion, I seized the dagger and placed the point on his breast, he never attempted to move.

"Wretch," cried I, "do not force me to murder you; I will plunge this blade into your heart if you do not at once tell me where my wife is."

He replied, in his calm way, "You are the master to do as you like, but with clasped hands I implore you to grant me one hour of life, and to follow me. Can you doubt him who thrice has owed his life to you, and whom you once called *brother*? Listen: if in one hour from this time you still doubt me, you shall be at perfect liberty to kill me. That will be time enough; you see that I do not attempt to resist you. I conjure you in the name of Maria—of your wife," he added slowly, as though the victim of some painful recollection, "give me but another hour, I beg of you, not for my sake, but for yours."

There was so much pathos in his entreaties that an inner feeling warned me to grant his request, and I yielded to that secret ascendency which he exercised over me, but which at that time I should have blushed to have confessed.

"Well," said I, slowly, "I will grant you one hour, and I am ready to follow you;" and as I spoke I handed him his dagger.

"No," answered he, "keep it; you still distrust me, but let us lose no time."

CHAPTER XLII.

Again we started. Rask, who, during our conversation, had shown frequent signs of impatience to renew his journey, bounded joyously before us. We plunged into a virgin forest, and after half an hour's walking we came out on a grassy opening in the wood. On one side was a waterfall dashing over rugged rocks, whilst the primeval trees of the forest surrounded it on all sides. Amongst the rocks was a cave, the grey face of which was shrouded by a mass of climbing plants. Rask ran towards it barking, but at a sign from Pierrot he became silent, and the latter taking me by the hand led me without a word to the entrance of the cave.

A woman with her back towards the light was seated on a mat: at the sound of our steps she turned——my friends——it was Marie! She wore the same white dress that she had done on the day of our marriage, and the wreath of orange blossoms was still on her head. She recognized me in a moment, and with a cry of joy threw herself into my arms. I was speechless with surprise and emotion. At her cry an old woman carrying a child in her arms hurried from an inner chamber formed in the depth of the cave, she was Marie's nurse, and she carried my uncle's youngest child.

Pierrot hastened to bring some water from the neighbouring spring, and threw a few drops in Marie's face, who was overcome by emotion; she speedily recovered, and opening her eyes, exclaimed—

"Leopold, my Leopold!"

"Marie," cried I, and my words were stifled in a kiss.

"Not before me, for pity's sake," cried a voice, in accents of agony.

We looked round; it came from Pierrot. The sight of our endearments appeared to inflict terrible torture on him, his bosom heaved, a cold perspiration bedewed his forehead, and every limb quivered. Suddenly he hid his face in his hands, and fled from the grotto repeating in tones of anguish—

"Not before me! not before me!"

Marie half raised herself in my arms, and following his retreating form with her eyes, exclaimed—

"Leopold, our happiness seems to trouble him; can it be that he loves me?"

The exclamation of the slave had showed that he was my rival, but Marie's speech proved that he was my trusty friend.

"Marie," answered I, as the wildest happiness mingled with the deepest regret filled my heart, "Marie, were you ignorant of it?"

"Until this moment I was," answered she, a blush overspreading her beautiful features. "Does he really love me, for he never let me know it."

I clasped her to my bosom, in all the madness of happiness.

"I have recovered both wife and friend; how happy am I, but how guilty, for I doubted him!"

"What!" cried Marie, in surprise, "had you doubts of Pierrot? oh, you have indeed been in fault. Twice has he saved my life, and perhaps more than life," she added, casting down her eyes; "without him the alligator would have devoured me, without him the negroes: it was Pierrot who rescued me from their hands, when they were about to send me to rejoin my unhappy father."

She broke off her speech with a flood of tears.

"And why," asked I, "did not Pierrot send you to Cap, to your husband?"

"He tried to do so," replied she, "but it was impossible, compelled as he was to conceal me both from the whites and the blacks, his position was a most difficult one; and then, too, he was ignorant where you were. Some said that they had seen you killed, but Pierrot assured me that this was not the case, and a something convinced me that he spoke the truth, for I felt that had you been dead, I should have died at the same time."

"Then, Pierrot brought you here?" asked I.

"Yes, my Leopold, this solitary cave is known only to him. At the same time that he rescued me, he saved all that remained alive of our family, my little brother and my old nurse, and hid us here."

"The place is very nice, and now that the war has destroyed our house, and ruined us, I should like to live here with you. Pierrot supplied all our wants. He used to come very often; he wore a plume of red feathers on his head. He used to console me by talking of you, and always assured me that we should meet again, but for the past three days I have not seen him, and I was beginning to be uneasy, when to-day he came back with you. He had been seeking for you, had he not?"

"Yes," replied I.

"But if so, how can he be in love with me? Are you sure of it?"

"Quite," answered I, "it was he who was about to stab me beneath your window, and spared me lest it should afflict you;

it was he who sang the love songs at the pavilion by the river."

"Then he is your rival," exclaimed Marie, with naïve surprise, "and the wicked man with the wild marigolds is Pierrot; I can hardly believe that. He was so respectful and humble to me, much more so than when he was our slave. It is true that sometimes he looked at me in a strange manner, but I attributed his sadness to our misfortunes. If you could only know with what tenderness he spoke of you, my Leopold. His friendship made him speak of you as much as my love did."

These explanations of Marie enchanted and yet grieved me. I felt how cruelly I had treated the noble-hearted Pierrot, and I felt all the force of his gentle reproach, *"It is not I who am ungrateful."*

At this instant Pierrot returned. His face was dark and gloomy, and he looked like a martyr returning from the place of torture, but yet retaining an air of triumph.

He came towards me, and pointing to the dagger in my belt, said—"The hour has passed!"

"Hour, what hour?" asked I.

"The one you granted me; it was necessary for me to have so much time allowed me in which to bring you here. Then I conjured you to spare my life, now I supplicate you to take it away."

The most tender feelings of the heart, love, gratitude, and friendship, united themselves together to torture me. Unable to say a word, but sobbing bitterly, I cast myself at the feet of the slave. He raised me up in haste.

"What are you doing?" cried he.

"I pay you the homage that is your due, but I am no longer worthy of friendship such as yours; can your friendship be pushed so far as to forgive me my ingratitude?"

For a time his expression remained stern, he appeared to be undergoing a violent mental contest. He took a step towards me; then drew back, and seemed on the point of speaking, but no words passed his lips. The struggle was a short one, he opened his arms to embrace me, saying—

"May I *now* call you brother?"

My only reply was to cast myself on his breast. After a short pause, he added—

"You were always kind, but misfortune had rendered you unjust."

"I have found my brother once again," said I. "I am unfortunate no longer, but I have been very guilty."

"Guilty, brother, I also have been guilty, and more so than you; you are no longer unhappy, but I shall be so for ever!"

CHAPTER XLIII.

The expression of pleasure which the renewal of our friendship had traced on his features, faded away and an appearance of deep grief once more pervaded them.

"Listen," said he, coldly; "my father was the King of Kakongo. Each day he sat at the door of his hut and dispensed justice amongst his subjects. After every judgment, according to the custom of the kings his ancestors, he drank a full goblet of palm wine. We were happy and powerful. But the Europeans came to our country; it was from them that I learnt the accomplishments which you appeared to be surprised at my possessing. Our principal acquaintance amongst the Europeans was a Spanish captain; he promised my father territories far greater than those he now ruled over, treasure, and white women; my father believed him, and gathering his family together, followed him.... Brother, he sold us as slaves!"

The breast of the negro rose and fell, as he strove to restrain himself; his eyes shot forth sparks of fire; and without seeming to know what he did, he broke in his powerful grasp a fancy medlar tree that stood beside him.

"The master of Kakongo in his turn had a master, and his son toiled as a slave in the furrows of Saint Domingo. They tore the young lion from his father, that they might the more easily tame him; they separated the wife from the husband, and the little children from the mother who nursed them, and the father who used to bathe them in the torrents of their native land. In their place they found cruel masters and a sleeping place shared with the dogs!"

He was silent, though his lips moved as though he were still continuing his narrative; after a moment's pause he seized me roughly by the arm, and continued—

"Brother, do you understand, I have been sold to different masters like a beast of burden? Do you remember the punishment of Ogé? it was on that day that I saw my father after a long separation—*he was on the wheel!*"

I shuddered; he went on—

"My wife was outraged by white men, and she died calling for revenge. Must I tell you I was guilty towards her, for I loved another; but let that pass by. All my people urged me to deliver and avenge them; Rask brought me their messages, I could do nothing for them, I was fast in your uncle's prison. The day upon which you obtained my release, I hurried off to save my children from the power of a cruel master. Upon the very day that I arrived, the last of the grandchildren of the King of Kakongo had expired under the blows of the white man; he had followed the others!"

He interrupted his recital, and coldly asked me:

"Brother, what would you have done?"

This frightful tale froze me with horror. I replied by a threatening gesture. He understood me, and with a bitter smile he continued—

"The slaves rose against their master, and punished the murder of my children. They chose me for their chief. You know the frightful excesses that were perpetrated by the insurgents. I heard that your uncle's slaves were on the point of rising. I arrived at Acul on the night upon which the insurrection broke out. You were away. Your uncle had been murdered in his bed, and the negroes had already set fire to the plantation. Not being able to restrain them—for in destroying your uncle's property they thought that they were avenging my injuries—I determined to save the survivors of his family. I entered the fort by the breach that I had made. I entrusted your wife's nurse to a faithful negro. I had more trouble in saving your Marie; she had hurried to the burning portion of the fort to save the youngest of her brothers, the sole survivor of the massacre. The insurgents surrounded her, and were about to kill her.... I burst upon them, and ordered them to leave her to my vengeance; they obeyed me, and retired. I took your wife in my arms, I entrusted the child to Rask, and I bore them both away to this cavern, of which I alone knew the existence and the access.

Brother, such was my crime."

More than ever overwhelmed with gratitude and remorse, I would again have thrown myself at his feet, but he stopped me.

"Come," said he, "take your wife, and let us leave this, all of us."

In wonder I asked him whither he wished to conduct us.

"To the camp of the whites," answered he. "This retreat is no longer safe. To-morrow at break of day the camp of Biassou will be attacked, and the forest will assuredly be set on fire. Besides, I have no time to lose. Ten lives are in jeopardy until my return. We *can* hasten because you are free; we *must* hasten because I am not."

These words increased my surprise, and I pressed him for an explanation.

"Have you not heard that Bug-Jargal is a prisoner?" replied he, impatiently.

"Yes; but what has Bug-Jargal to do with you?"

In his turn he seemed astonished, and then in a grave voice he answered—

"*I am Bug-Jargal.*"

CHAPTER XLIV.

I had thought that nothing that related to this extraordinary man could have surprised me. I had experienced some feelings of astonishment in finding the slave Pierrot transformed into an African King, but my admiration reached its height, when from his own confession I learned that he was the courageous, and magnanimous Bug-Jargal, the chief of the insurgents of Morne-Rouge; and I understood the respectful demeanour shown by all the rebels, even by Biassou, to Bug-Jargal, the King of Kakongo. He did not notice the impression that his last words had made upon me.

"They told me," continued he, "that you were a prisoner in Biassou's camp, and I hastened to deliver you."

"But you told me just now that you too were a prisoner."

He glanced inquisitively at me, as though seeking my reason for putting this natural question.

"Listen," answered he. "This morning I was a prisoner in the hands of your friends, but I heard a report that Biassou had announced his intention of executing, before sunset to-day, a young prisoner named Leopold d'Auverney. They doubled my guards, and I was informed that my execution would immediately follow yours, and that in the event of escape, ten of my comrades would suffer in my stead. So you see that I have no time to lose."

I still detained him.

"You made your escape then?" asked I.

"How else could I have been here? it was necessary to save you. Did I not owe you my life? Come, let us set out, we are an hour's march from the camp of the whites, and about the same distance from that of Biassou. See the shadow of the cocoa-nut trees are lengthening, and their round tops look on the pass like the egg of the giant condor. In three hours the sun will have set. Come, brother, time waits for no man."

In three hours the sun will have set! These words froze my blood, like an apparition from the tomb. They recalled to my mind the fatal promise which bound me to Biassou. Alas! in the rapture of seeing Marie again, I had not thought of our approaching eternal separation. I had been overwhelmed with my happiness, a flood of joyful emotions had swept away my memory, and in the midst of my delight I had forgotten that the inexorable finger of death was beckoning to me. But the words of my friend recalled everything to my mind. *In three hours the sun will have set!* It would take an hour to reach Biassou's camp. There could be no faltering with my duty. The villain had my word, and it would never do to give him the chance of despising what he seemed still to put trust in—the word of a Frenchman; better far to die. The alternative was a terrible one, and I confess that I hesitated for a moment before I chose the right course. Can you blame me, gentlemen?

CHAPTER XLV.

With a deep sigh, I placed one hand in that of Bug-Jargal, and the other in that of Marie, who gazed with anxiety on the sadness that had overspread my features.

"Bug-Jargal," said I, struggling with emotion, "I entrust to you the only being in the world that I love more than you—my Marie. Return to the camp without me, for I may not follow you."

"Great heavens!" exclaimed Marie, hardly able to breathe from her terror and anxiety, "what new misfortune is this?"

Bug-Jargal trembled, and a look of mingled sorrow and

surprise passed over his face.

"Brother, what is this that you say?"

The terror that had seized upon Marie at the thought of the coming misfortune which her love for me had almost caused her to divine, made me determined to spare her the dreadful truth for the moment. I placed my mouth to Bug-Jargal's ear, and whispered in hurried accents: "I am a prisoner. I swore to Biassou that two hours before sunset I would once more place myself in his hands; in fact, I have sworn to return to my death!"

Filled with rage, in a loud voice he exclaimed:

"The monster! This then was his motive for a secret interview with you—it was to bind you with this fatal promise. I ought to have distrusted the wretch. Why did I not foresee that there must be some treachery lurking in the request, for he is a mulatto, not a black."

"What is this—what treachery? what promise?" said Marie, in an agony of terror. "And who is Biassou?"

"Silence, silence," repeated I, in a low voice to Bug-Jargal; "do not let us alarm Marie."

"Good," answered he; "but why did you give such a pledge, how could you consent?"

"I thought that you had deceived me, and that Marie was lost to me for ever. What was life to me then?"

"But a simple promise cannot bind you to a brigand like that."

"I gave my word of honour."

He did not seem to understand me.

"Your word of honour," repeated he; "but what is that? You did not drink out of the same cup; you have not broken a ring together, or a branch of the red-blossomed maple?"

"No, we have done none of these things."

"Well, then, what binds you to him?"

"My honour!"

"I cannot understand you; nothing pledges you to Biassou; come with us?"

"I cannot, my brother, for I am bound by my promise."

"No, you are not bound," cried he, angrily. "Sister, add your prayers to mine, and entreat your husband not to leave you. He wishes to return to the negro camp from which I rescued him, on the plea that he has promised to place his life in Biassou's hands."

"What have you done?" cried I.

It was too late to stay the effects of the generous impulse that had prompted him to endeavour to save the life of his rival by the help of her he loved. Marie cast herself into my arms with a cry of anguish, her hands clasped my neck, and she hung upon my breast, speechless and breathless.

"Oh, my Leopold, what does he say?" murmured she, at last. "Is he not deceiving me? It is not immediately after our reunion that you must quit me again. Answer me quickly or I shall die. You have no right to throw away your life, for you have given it to me. You would not leave me, never to see me again."

"Marie," answered I, "we shall meet again, but it will be in another place."

"In another place! Where?" she asked, in faltering accents.

"In heaven," I answered; for to this angel I could not lie.

Again she fainted, but this time it was from grief. I raised her up, and placed her in the arms of Bug-Jargal, whose eyes were full of tears.

"Nothing can keep you back, then," said he; "I will add nothing to my entreaties, this sight ought to be enough. How can you resist Marie? For one word like she has spoken I would have sacrificed the world, and you cannot even give up death for her."

"Honour binds me," answered I, sadly. "Farewell, Bug-Jargal, farewell, brother; I leave her to you."

He grasped my hand, overwhelmed with grief, and appeared hardly to understand me.

"Brother," said he, "in the camp of the whites there are some of your relations, I will give her over to them; for my part I cannot accept your legacy."

He pointed to a rocky crag which towered high above the adjacent country.

"Do you see that rock?" asked he, "when the signal of your death shall float from it, it will promptly be answered by the volley that announces mine."

Hardly understanding his last words, I embraced him, pressed a last kiss upon the pale lips of Marie, who was slowly recovering under the attentions of her nurse, and fled precipitately, fearing that another look or word would shake my resolution.

CHAPTER XLVI.

I fled away, and plunged into the depths of the forest, following the tracks that we had left but a short time before, and not daring to cast a last glance behind me.

To stifle the grief which oppressed my heart, I dashed, without a moment's pause, through the thickets, past hill and plain, until I reached the crest of a rock from which I could see the camp of Biassou, with its lines of waggons and huts swarming with life, and looking in the distance like a vast ant-hill.

Then I halted, for I felt that I had reached the end of my journey, and my life at the same time. Fatigue and emotion had weakened my physical powers, and I leaned against a tree to save myself from falling, and allowed my eyes to wander over the plain, which was to be my place of execution.

Up to this moment I had imagined that I had drained the cup of bitterness and gall to the dregs, but I had not until then tasted the most cruel of all misfortunes, that of being constrained by powerful moral force to voluntarily renounce life when it appeared most sweet. Some hours before I cared not for the world; extreme despair is a simulation of death which makes the reality more earnestly desired.

Marie had been restored to me, my dead happiness had been resuscitated, my past had become my future, and all my overshadowed hopes had beamed forth more gloriously than ever, and again had a new life, a life of youth, and love, and enchantment, showed gloriously upon the horizon. I was ready to enter upon this life, everything invited me to it; no material obstacle, no hindrance, was apparent; I was free, I was happy, and yet—I was about to die. I had made but one step into paradise and a hidden duty compelled me to retrace it, and to enter upon a path the goal of which was Death!

Death has but few terrors for the crushed and broken spirit, but how heavy and icy is his hand when it grasps the heart which has just begun to live and revel in the joys of life. I felt that I had emerged from the tomb, and had for a moment enjoyed the greatest delights of life, love, friendship, and liberty, and now the door of the sepulchre was again opened, and an unseen force compelled me once more to enter it for ever.

CHAPTER XLVII.

When the first bitter pang of grief had passed, a kind of fury took possession of me, and I entered the valley with a rapid step, for I felt the necessity of shortening the period of suspense. When I presented myself at the negro outpost the sergeant in command at first refused to permit me to pass. It seemed strange that I should have had to have recourse to entreaties to enable me to effect my object. At last two of them seized me by the arms and led me into Biassou's presence.

As I entered the grotto he was engaged in examining the springs of various instruments of torture with which he was surrounded. At the noise my guard made in introducing me he turned his head, but my presence did not seem to surprise him.

"Do you see these?" asked he, displaying the horrible engines which lay before him.

I remained calm and impassive, for I knew the cruel nature of the *hero of humanity*, and I was determined to endure to the end without blenching.

"Leogri was lucky in being only hung, was he not?" asked he, with his sardonic sneer.

I gazed upon him with cold disdain, but I made no reply.

"Tell his reverence the chaplain that the prisoner has returned," said he to an aide-de-camp.

During the absence of the negro, we both remained silent, but I could see that he watched me narrowly.

Just then Rigaud entered, he seemed agitated, and whispered a few words to the general.

"Summon the chiefs of the different bands," said Biassou, calmly.

A quarter of an hour afterwards, the different chiefs in their strange equipments, were assembled in the grotto. Biassou rose.

"Listen to me, friends and comrades, the whites will attack us here at daybreak, our position is a bad one, and we must quit it. At sunset we will march to the Spanish frontier; Macaya, you and your negroes will form the advanced guards; Padrejan, see that the guns taken at Pralato are spiked, we cannot take them into the mountains; the brave men of Croix-des-Bouquets will follow Macaya; Toussaint will come next with the blacks from Léogane and Trose. If the *griots* or the*griotes* make any disturbance, I will hand them over to the executioner of the army. Lieutenant-Colonel Cloud will distribute the English muskets that were disembarked at Cape Cabron, and will lead the half-breeds through the byways of the Vista. Slaughter any prisoners that may remain, notch the bullets, and poison the arrows. Let three tons of arsenic be thrown into the wells; the colonists will take it for sugar, and drink without distrust. Block up the roads to the plain with rocks, line the hedges with marksmen, and set fire to the forest. Rigaud, you will remain with me; Candi, summon my body-guard. The negroes of

Morne-Rouge will form the rear-guard, and will not evacuate the camp until sunrise."

He leaned over to Rigaud, and whispered hoarsely—

"They are Bug-Jargal's men; if they are killed, all the better. 'Muerta la tropa, muerte el gefe!' ('If the men die, the chief will die.') Go, my brethren," he added, rising, "you will receive instructions from Candi."

The chiefs left the grotto.

"General," remarked Rigaud, "we ought to send that dispatch of Jean François; affairs are going badly, and it would stop the advance of the whites."

Biassou drew it hastily from his pocket.

"I agree with you, but there are so many faults, both in grammar and spelling, that they will laugh at it."

He presented the paper to me.

"For the last time, will you save your life? My kindness gives you a last chance. Help me to correct this letter, and to re-write it in proper official style."

I shook my head.

"Do you mean no?" asked he.

"I do," I replied.

"Reflect," he answered, with a sinister glance at the instruments of torture.

"It is because I have reflected that I refuse," replied I. "You are alarmed for the safety of yourself and your men, and you count upon this letter to delay the just vengeance of the whites. I do not desire to retain a life which may perhaps have saved yours. Let my execution commence."

"Ha, boy," exclaimed Biassou, touching the instruments of torture with his foot, "you are growing familiar with these, are you? I am sorry, but I have not the time to try them on you. Our position is a dangerous one, and we must get out of it as soon as we can. And so you refuse to act as my secretary? Well, you are right, for it would not after all have saved your miserable life, which, by the way, I have promised to his reverence my chaplain. Do you think that I would permit any one to live who holds the secrets of Biassou?"

He turned to the Obi, who just then entered.

"Good father, is your guard ready?"

The latter made a sign in the affirmative.

"Have you taken it from amongst the negroes of Morne-Rouge? for they are the only ones who are not occupied in preparations for departure."

Again the Obi bowed his head.

Then Biassou pointed out to me the black flag which I had before remarked in a corner of the grotto.

"That will show your friends when the time comes to give your place to your lieutenant. But I have no more time to lose, I must be off. By the way, you have been for a little excursion; how did you like the neighbourhood?"

"I noticed that there were enough trees upon which to hang you and all your band."

"Ah," retorted he, with his hideous laugh, "there is one place that you have not seen, but with which the good father will make you acquainted. Adieu, my young captain, and give my compliments to Leogri."

He bade me farewell with a chuckle that reminded me of the hiss of the rattlesnake, and turned his back as the negroes dragged me away.

The veiled Obi followed us, his rosary in his hand.

CHAPTER XLVIII.

I walked between my guards without offering any resistance, which would indeed have been hopeless; we ascended the shoulder of a hill on the western side of the plain, and then my escort sat down for a brief period of repose. As we did so I cast a last lingering look at the setting sun which would never rise again for me on this earth.

My guards rose to their feet, and I followed their example, and we descended into a little dell, the beauty of which under any other circumstances would have filled me with admiration. A mountain stream ran through the bottom of the dell, which by its refreshing coolness produced a thick and luxuriant growth of vegetation, and fell into one of those dark blue lakes with which the hills of St. Domingo abound. How often in happier days have I sat and dreamed on the borders of these beautiful lakes in the twilight hour, when beneath the influence of the moon their deep azure changed into a sheet of silver, or when the reflections of the stars sowed the surface with a thousand golden spangles! How lovely this valley appeared to me! There were magnificent plane-trees of gigantic growth, closely grown thickets of *mauritias*, a kind of palm, which allows no other vegetation to flourish beneath its shade, date-trees, and magnolias with the goblet-shaped flowers, the tall catalpa, with its polished and exquisitely chiselled blossoms, standing out in relief against the golden buds of the ebony-trees. The Canadian maple mingled its yellow flowers with the blue aureolas of that species of the wild honeysuckle which the negroes call *coali*. Thick curtains of luxurious creepers concealed the bare sides of the rocks, whilst from the virgin soil rose a soft perfume, such as the first man may have inhaled amidst Eden's groves.

We continued our way along a footpath traced on the brink of the torrent. I was surprised to notice that this path closed abruptly at the foot of a tall peak, in which was a natural archway, from which flowed a rapid torrent.

A dull roar of falling waters, and an impetuous wind issued from this natural tunnel. The negroes who escorted me took a path to the left which led into a cavern and seemed to be the bed of a torrent that had long been dried up. Overhead I could see the rugged roof, half hidden by masses of vegetation, and the same sound of falling waters filled the whole of the vault. As I took the first step into the cavern, the Obi came to my side, and whispered in a hoarse voice, "Listen to what I have to predict: one of us two only shall leave by this path and issue again from the entrance of the cave."

I disdained to make any reply, and we advanced further into the gloom.

The noise became louder, and drowned the sound of our footfalls. I fancied that there must be a waterfall near, and I was not deceived.

After moving through the darkness for nearly ten minutes, we found ourselves on a kind of internal platform caused by the central formation of the mountain. The larger portion of this platform, which was of a semicircular shape, was inundated by a torrent which burst from the interior of the mountain with a terrible din. Above this subterranean hall the roof rose into the shape of a dome, covered with moss of a yellowish hue. A large opening was formed in the dome through which the daylight penetrated, and the sides of the crevice were fringed with green trees, gilded just now by the last rays of the setting sun. At the northern extremity of the platform the torrent fell with a frightful noise into a deep abyss, over which appeared to float, without being able to illuminate its depths, a feeble portion of the light which came through the aperture in the roof. Over this terrible precipice hung the trunk of an old tree whose topmost branches were filled with the foam of the waterfall, and whose knotty roots pierced through the rock two or three feet below the brink.

This tree, whose top and roots were both swept by the torrent, hung over the abyss like a skeleton arm, and was so destitute of foliage that I could not distinguish its species. It had a strange and weird appearance; the humidity which saturated its roots prevented it from dying, whilst the force of the cataract tore off its new shoots, and only left it with the branches that had strength to resist the force of the water.

CHAPTER XLIX.

In this terrible spot the negroes came to a halt, and I knew that my hour had come.

It was in this abyss, then, that was to be sunk all my hopes in this world. The image of the happiness which but a few hours before I had voluntarily renounced, brought to my heart a feeling of regret, almost one of remorse.

To pray for mercy was unworthy of me, but I could not refrain from giving utterance to my regrets.

"Friends," said I to the negroes who surrounded me, "it is a sad thing to die at twenty years of age, full of life and strength, when one is loved by one whom in your turn you adore, and you leave behind you eyes that will even weep for your untimely end."

A mocking burst of laughter hailed my expression of regret. It came from the little Obi. This species of evil spirit, this living mystery, approaches me roughly.

"Ha, ha, ha! you regret life then, *Labadosca Dios*. My only fear was that death would have no terrors for you."

It was the same voice, the same laugh that had so often before baffled my conjectures.

"Wretch!" exclaimed I, "who *are* you?"

"You are going to learn," replied he, in a voice of concentrated passion; and thrusting aside the silver sun that half concealed his brown chest, he exclaimed, "Look!" I bent forward.

Two names were written in white letters on the hairy chest of the Obi, showing but too clearly the hideous and ineffaceable brand of the heated iron. One of these names was *Effingham*, the other was that of my uncle and myself, *D'Auverney*!

I was struck dumb with surprise.

"Well, Leopold d'Auverney," asked the Obi, "does not your name tell you mine?"

"No," answered I, astonished to hear the man name me, and seeking to recall to my mind my thoughts. "These two names were only to be found thus united upon the chest of my uncle's fool. But the poor dwarf is dead, and besides that, he was devotedly attached to us. You cannot be Habibrah."

"No other," shrieked he, and casting aside the blood-stained cap, he raised his veil and showed me the hideous features of the household fool; but a threatening and sinister expression had usurped the half-imbecile smile which was formerly eternally imprinted on his features.

"Great God!" exclaimed I, overwhelmed with surprise, "do all the dead, then, come back to life! It is Habibrah, my uncle's fool."

"His fool—and also his murderer."

I recoiled from him in horror.

"His murderer, wretch—was it thus that you repaid his kindness?"

He interrupted me.

"His kindness! rather say his insults."

"What!" I again cried, "was it you, villain, who struck the fatal blow?"

"It was," he replied, with a terrible expression upon his face. "I plunged my knife so deeply into his heart that he had hardly time to cast aside sleep before death claimed him. He cried out feebly, 'Habibrah, come to me,' *but I was with him* already."

The cold-blooded manner in which he narrated the murder disgusted me.

"Wretch! cowardly assassin! You forgot, then, all his kindness, that you ate at his table, and slept at the foot of his bed——"

"Like a dog," interrupted Habibrah, roughly, "*como un perro.* I thought too much of what you call his kindness, but which I looked upon as insults. I took vengeance upon him, and I will do the same to you. Listen: do you think that because I am a mulatto and a deformed dwarf that I am not a man? Ah, I have a soul stronger, deeper, and bolder than the one that I am about to set free from your girlish frame. I was given to your uncle as if I had been a pet monkey. I was his butt, I amused him, whilst he despised me. He loved me, do you say—yes, forsooth, I had a place in his heart between his dog and his parrot, but I found a better place there with my dagger." I shuddered.

"Yes," continued the dwarf, "it was I, I that did it all. Look me well in the face, Leopold d'Auverney; you have often laughed at me, now you shall tremble before me. And you dare to speak of your uncle's liking for me, a liking that carried degradation with it. If I entered the room a shout of contemptuous laughter was my greeting; my appearance, my deformities, my features, my costume—all furnished food for laughter to your accursed uncle and his accursed friends, whilst I was not allowed to remain silent, it was necessary for me to join in the laughter that was levelled at me; I foam with rage whilst I think of it.

"Answer me: do you think that after such humiliations I could feel anything but the deadliest hatred for the creature that inflicted them upon me? Do you not think that they were a thousand times harder to endure than the toil in the burning sun, the fetters, and the whip of the driver, which were the lot of the other slaves? Do you not think that they would cause ardent, implacable, and eternal hatred to spring up in the heart of man as lasting as the accursed brand which degrades my chest? Has not the vengeance that I have taken for my sufferings been short and insufficient. Why could I not make my tyrant suffer but a small portion of what I endured for so many years? Why could he not before his death know the bitterness of wounded pride, and feel what burning traces tears of shame leave upon a face condemned to wear a perpetual smile? Alas! it is too hard to have waited so long for the hour of vengeance, and then only to find it in a dagger thrust! Had he but only known the hand that struck him it would have been something; but I was too eager to hear his dying groan, and I drove the knife too quickly home; he died without having recognized me, and my eagerness baulked my vengeance. This time at least, however, it shall be more complete. You see me, do you not? though in point of fact you may be unable to recognize me in my new character. You have always been in the habit of seeing me laughing and joyous, but now nothing prevents me from letting my true nature appear on my face, and I do not greatly resemble my former self. You only knew my mask; look upon my real face!"

At that moment his appearance was truly terrible.

"Monster," exclaimed I, "you deceive yourself; there is more of buffoonery than heroism in your face even now, and nothing in your heart but cruelty."

"Do not speak of cruelty," retorted he, "think of your uncle——"

"Wretch," returned I, "if he were cruel it was at your instigation. You, to pretend to pity the position of the poor slaves—why, then, did you exert all your influence to make their master treat them less harshly? Why did you never intercede in their favour?"

"I would not have done so for the world. Would I ever attempt to hinder a white man from blackening his soul by an act of cruelty? No, no, I urged him to inflict more and more punishment upon them, so as to hurry on the revolt, and so draw down a surer vengeance upon the heads of our oppressors.

In seeming to injure my brethren I was serving them."

I was thunderstruck at such a cunning act of diplomacy carried out by such a man.

"Well," continued the dwarf, "do you believe now that I had the brain to conceive and the hand to execute? What do you think of Habibrah the buffoon? what do you think of your uncle's fool?"

"Finish what you have begun so well," replied I. "Let me die, but let there be no more delay."

"And suppose I wish for delay? Suppose that it does my heart good to watch you in the agonies of suspense? You see Biassou owed me my share in the last plunder. When I saw you in our camp I asked for your life as my share, and he granted it willingly, and now you are mine; I am amusing myself with you. Soon you will follow the stream of the cataract into the abyss beneath; but before doing so let me tell you that I have discovered the spot where your wife is concealed, and it was I that advised Biassou to set the forest on fire; and the work, I imagine, is already begun. Thus your family will be swept from the face of the earth. Your uncle fell by steel, you will perish by water, and your Marie by fire!"

"Villain! villain!" I exclaimed, and I made an effort to seize him by the throat, but a wave of his hand summoned my guards.

"Bind him!" cried he; "he precipitates his hour of doom!" In dead silence the negroes commenced to bind me with the cords that they had carried with them. Suddenly I fancied that I heard the distant barking of a dog, but this sound might be only an illusion caused by the noise of the cascade.

The negroes had finished binding me, and placed me on the brink of the abyss into which I was so soon to be hurled.

The dwarf with folded arms gazed upon the scene with a sinister expression of joy.

I lifted my eyes to the opening in the roof so as to avoid the triumphant expression of malice painted on his countenance, and to take one last look at the blue sky. At that instant the barking was more distinctly heard, and the enormous head of Rask appeared at the opening.

I trembled; the dwarf exclaimed, "Finish with him!" and the negroes, who had not noticed the dog, raised me in their arms to hurl me into the hell of waters which roared and foamed beneath me.

CHAPTER L.

"Comrades!" cried a voice of thunder.

All looked at the spot from whence the sound proceeded: Bug-Jargal was standing on the edge of the opening, a crimson plume floating on his head.

"Comrades," repeated he, "stay your hands!"

The negroes prostrated themselves upon the earth in token of submission.

"I am Bug-Jargal," continued he.

The negroes struck the earth with their heads, uttering cries the meaning of which I could not comprehend.

"Unbind the prisoner," commanded the chief.

But now the dwarf appeared to recover from the stupor into which the sudden appearance of Bug-Jargal had thrown him, and seized by the arm the negro who was preparing to cut the cords that bound me.

"What is the meaning of this? What are you doing?" cried he.

Then, raising his voice, he addressed Bug-Jargal: "Chief of Morne-Rouge," cried he, "what are you doing here?"

"I have come to command my own men," was the reply.

"Yes," answered the dwarf, in tones of concentrated passion, "these negroes do certainly belong to your band; but," added he, raising his voice again, "by what right do you interfere with my prisoner?"

The chief answered, "I am Bug-Jargal;" and again the negroes struck the ground with their foreheads.

"Bug-Jargal," continued Habibrah, "cannot contravene the orders of Biassou; this white man was given to me by Biassou; I desire his death, and die he shall. Obey me," he added, turning to the negroes, "and hurl him into the abyss."

At the well-known voice of the Obi the negroes rose to their feet and took a step towards me. I thought all was lost.

"Unbind the prisoner!" cried Bug-Jargal again.

In an instant I was free. My surprise was equalled by the fury of the Obi. He attempted to throw himself upon me. The negroes interfered; then he burst out into imprecations and threats.

" 'Demonios! rabia! inferno de mi alma!' How, wretches, you refuse to obey me! Do you not recognize my voice! Why did I lose time in talking to this accursed one? I ought to have had him hurled without delay to the fishes of the gulf. By wishing to make my vengeance more complete I have lost it all together. *Orabia de Satan*. Listen to me: if you do not obey me, and hurl him into the abyss, I will curse you; your hair shall grow white, the mosquitoes and sandflies shall eat you up alive, your legs and your arms shall bend like reeds, your breath shall burn your throat like red hot-sand, you shall die young, and after your death your spirits shall be compelled to turn a millstone as big as a mountain, in the moon where it is always cold."

The scene was a strange one. The only one of my colour, in a damp and gloomy cavern surrounded by negroes with the aspect of demons, balanced as it were upon the edge of a bottomless gulf, and every now and then threatened by a deformed dwarf, by a hideous sorcerer upon whose striped garments and pointed cap the fading light shone faintly, yet protected by a tall negro who was standing at the only point from which daylight could be seen, it appeared to me that I was at the gates of hell, awaiting the conflict between my good and evil angels, to result in the salvation or the destruction of my soul. The negroes appeared to be terrified at the threats of the Obi, and he endeavoured to profit by their indecision.

"I desire the death of the white man, and he *shall* die; obey me."

Bug-Jargal replied solemnly, "He shall live; I am Bug-Jargal, my father was the King of Kakongo, who dispensed justice at the gate of his palace."

Again the negroes cast themselves upon the ground.

The chief continued.

"Brethren, go and tell Biassou not to unfurl the black banner upon the mountain-top which should announce to the whites the signal of this man's death, for he was the saviour of Bug-Jargal's life, and Bug-Jargal wills that he should live."

They rose up. Bug-Jargal threw his red plume on the ground

before them. The chief of the guard picked it up with every show of respect, and they left the cavern without a word; whilst the Obi, with a glance of rage, followed them down the subterranean avenue.

I will not attempt to describe my feelings at that moment. I fixed my eyes, wet with tears, upon Pierrot, who gazed upon me with a singular expression of love and tenderness. "God be praised," said he, "you are saved. Brother, go back by the road by which you entered, you will meet me again in the valley."

He waved his hand to me and disappeared from my sight.

CHAPTER LI.

Eager to arrive at the appointed meeting-place, and to learn by what fortunate means my saviour had been enabled to make his appearance at so opportune a moment, I prepared to leave the cavern in which my nerves had been so severely tried; but as I prepared to enter the subterranean passage an unexpected obstacle presented itself in my path.

It was Habibrah!

The revengeful Obi had not in reality followed the negroes as I had believed, but had concealed himself behind a rocky projection of the cave, waiting for a propitious moment for his vengeance; and this moment had come. He laughed bitterly as he showed himself. A dagger, the same that he was in the habit of using for a crucifix, shone in his right hand: at the sight of it I recoiled a step.

"Ha, accursed one, did you think to escape me? But the fool is not such a fool after all! I have you, and this time there shall be no delay. Your friend Bug-Jargal shall not wait for you long, you shall soon be at the meeting-place, but it will be the wave of the cataract that shall bear you there."

As he spoke he dashed at me with uplifted weapon.

"Monster," cried I, retreating to the platform, "just now you were only an executioner, now you are a murderer."

"I am an avenger," returned he, grinding his teeth.

I was on the edge of the precipice; he endeavoured to hurl me over with a blow of his dagger. I avoided it. His foot slipped on the treacherous moss which covered the rocks, he rolled into the slope polished and rounded by the constant flow of water.

"A thousand devils!" roared he.

He had fallen into the abyss.

I have already mentioned that the roots of the old tree projected through the crevices of the rocks, a little below the edge of the precipice. In his fall the dwarf struck against these, his striped petticoat caught in them, he grasped at them as a last hope of safety, and clung to them with all the energy of despair.

His pointed bonnet fell from his head; to maintain his position he had to let go his dagger, and the two together disappeared in the depths of the abyss.

Habibrah, suspended over the terrible gulf, strove vainly to regain the platform, but his short arms could not reach the rocky edge, and he broke his nails in useless efforts to obtain a hold on the muddy surface of the rocks which sloped down into the terrible abyss.

He howled with rage.

The slightest push on my part would have been sufficient to hurl him to destruction, but it would have been an act of cowardice, and I made no movement. This moderation on my part seemed to surprise him.

Thanking heaven for its mercies, I determined to abandon him to his fate, and was about to leave the cave when, in a voice broken with fear, and which appeared to come from the depths of the abyss, he addressed me.

"Master," cried he, "master, do not go, for pity's sake! do not, in the name of heaven, leave a guilty creature to perish, that it is in your power to save. Alas, my strength is failing me; the roots bend, and slip through my fingers, the weight of my body drags me down—I must let go, or my arms will break! Alas, master, the fearful gulfs boils and seethes beneath me! *Nombre santo de Dios!* Have you no pity for the poor fool? He has been very guilty, but prove that the white men are better than the mulattoes, the masters than the slaves, by saving him."

I approached the brink of the precipice, and the feeble light that broke through the aperture in the roof showed me, on the repulsive features of the dwarf, an expression which I had never noticed before, that of prayer and supplication.

"Señor Leopold," continued he, encouraged by the movement of pity that I showed, "can you see a fellow-creature in so terrible a position of peril, without stretching out a hand to save him? Give me your hand, master; with very slight assistance from you I can save myself—I only ask for a little help. Help me then, and my gratitude shall be as great as my crimes."

I interrupted him.

"Unhappy wretch, do not recall them to my memory."

"It is because I repent of them that I do so. Oh, be generous to me! O heavens, my hand relaxes its grasp, and I fall! *Ay desdichado!* The hand, your hand; in the name of the mother who bore you, give me your hand!"

I cannot describe the tone of agony in which he pleaded for help. In this moment of peril I forgot all; it was no longer an enemy, a traitor, and an assassin, but an unhappy fellow-creature, whom a slight exertion upon my part could rescue from a frightful death. He implored me in heart-rending accents. Reproaches would have been fruitless, and out of place. The necessity for help was urgent and immediate. I stooped, knelt down on the brink of the precipice, and grasping the trunk of the tree with one hand, I extended the other to Habibrah.

As soon as it was within his reach, he grasped it with both his hands, and hung on to it with all his strength. Far from attempting to aid me in my efforts to draw him up, I felt that he was exerting all his powers to draw me down with him into the abyss. If it had not been for the assistance afforded to me by the trunk of the tree, I must infallibly have been dragged over by the violent and unexpected jerk that the wretched man gave me.

"Villain!" cried I; "what are you doing?"

"Avenging myself," answered he, with a peal of devilish laughter. "Aha! madman, have I got you in my clutches once more? You have of your own free-will placed yourself again in my power, and I hold you tight. You were saved and I was lost, and yet you of your own accord place your head between the jaws of the alligator, because it wept after having roared. I can bear death, since it will give me revenge. You are caught in the trap, *amigo*, and I shall take a companion with me to feed the fishes of the lake."

"Ah, traitor!" cried I, struggling with all my strength. "Is it thus that you serve me when I was trying to save you?"

"Yes," hissed he. "I know that we could have saved ourselves together, but I would rather that we should die at the same moment. I had rather compass your death, than save my life. Come down!"

As he spoke, his brown muscular hands grasped mine with unexpected strength, his eyes blazed, his mouth foamed; the strength, the departure of which he had before so piteously bewailed, had returned to him increased a thousandfold by the hope of revenge. His feet were planted like two perpendicular levers on a ledge of rock, and he struggled like a tiger against the root which, entangled in his clothes, supported him in spite of himself, for he was endeavouring with all his might to shake himself free, so as to bring all his weight to bear on me, and to drag me more quickly into the yawning gulf below.

In his rage he endeavoured to bite me, whilst his hideous features were rendered more terrible by their expression of satanic frenzy.

He looked like the demon of the cave seeking to drag down his victim to his abode of gloom and darkness.

One of my knees, by good fortune, was planted in a groove of the rock, and my arm was wrapped round the trunk of the tree, and I strove against the efforts of the dwarf with all the strength that the feeling of self-preservation could give me at such a moment.

Every now and then I drew a long breath, and shouted "Bug-Jargal" with all the force of my lungs. But the roar of the cascade, and the distance that he must be off, gave me but faint hopes of my voice reaching him.

But the dwarf, who had not anticipated so vigorous a resistance on my part, redoubled his efforts. I began to grow weak, though in reality the struggle had not taken so long as the narration of it. A violent pain paralyzed my arm, my sight grew dim, bright sparks flashed before my eyes, and a buzzing sound filled my ears. I heard the creaking of the root as it bent, mingled with the laugh of the monster, and the abyss seemed to rise up towards me as though eager to engulf its prey. But before I gave up all hope I made a last effort, and collecting together my exhausted forces, I once again shouted "Bug-Jargal."

A loud bark replied to me; it was Rask who thus answered my appeal for help. I glanced upwards—Bug-Jargal and his dog were gazing at me from the orifice in the roof.

He saw my danger at once.

"Hold on!" cried he.

Habibrah, fearing that I might yet be saved, foamed with rage, and crying, "Come down there, come down!" renewed the attack with almost supernatural vigour.

At this moment, weakened by the long struggle, my arm lost its hold of the tree. All seemed over with me, when I felt myself seized from behind. It was Rask!

At a sign from his master he had leapt down on the platform, and seized me by the skirts of my uniform with his powerful teeth.

This unlooked-for aid saved me. Habibrah had exhausted all his strength in a last convulsive effort, whilst I put forth all mine and succeeded in withdrawing my hand from his cramped and swollen fingers. The root, which had been for some time yielding, now parted suddenly, Rask gave me a violent pull backwards, and the wretched dwarf disappeared in the foam of the cascade, hurling a curse at me which was swallowed up with him in the whirl of waters.

Such was the terrible end of my uncle's fool.

CHAPTER LII.

The excitement of the last few hours, the terrible struggle and its awful conclusion, had utterly exhausted me, and I lay where I had fallen, almost deprived of sense or power of motion. The voice of Bug-Jargal restored me to myself.

"Brother," cried he, "hasten to leave this place. In half an hour the sun will have set; I will meet you in the valley. Follow Rask."

The words of my friend restored hope, strength, and courage to me. I rose to my feet. The great dog ran rapidly down the subterranean passage; I followed him, his bark guiding me through the darkness. After a time I saw a streak of light, and in a few minutes I gained the entrance, and breathed more freely as I passed through the archway. As I left the damp and gloomy vault behind me, I recalled to my mind the prediction of the dwarf, and its fatal fulfilment, "*One only of us shall return by this road.*" His attempt had failed, but the prophecy had been carried out.

CHAPTER LIII.

Bug-Jargal was waiting for me in the valley. I threw myself into his arms, but I had so many questions to put to him that I could not find words in which to express them.

"Listen to me," said he. "Your wife, my sister, is in safety in the camp of the white men; I handed her over to a relation of yours who was in command of the outposts, and I wished to again constitute myself a prisoner, lest they should execute the ten prisoners whose lives were security for my reappearance. But your relative told me to return, and, if possible, to prevent your execution; and that the ten negroes should not be executed until Biassou should announce the fact by displaying a black flag on one of the highest peaks of the mountains. Then I returned to do my best. Rask led me to where you were—thanks be to heaven, I arrived in time. You will live, and so shall I."

He extended his hand to me, adding—

"Brother, are you satisfied?"

I again clasped him to my breast; I entreated him not to leave me again, but to remain with the white troops, and I promised him to exert all my influence to procure him a commission in the colonial army. But he interrupted me with an angry air.

"Brother," asked he, "do I propose to you to join my army?"

I kept silence, for I felt that I had been guilty of a folly; then he added in a tone of affected gaiety—

"Come, let us hurry to the camp to reassure your wife."

This proposal was what I most ardently desired; we started at once. The negro knew the way, and took the lead; Rask followed us.

Here D'Auverney stopped suddenly, and cast a gloomy look around him; perspiration in large beads covered his forehead; he concealed his face with his hands. Rask looked at him with an air of uneasiness.

"Yes, you may well look at me like that," murmured he.

An instant afterwards he rose from his seat in a state of violent agitation, and, followed by the sergeant and the dog, rushed hurriedly from the tent.

CHAPTER LIV.

"I will lay a bet," said Henri, "that we are nearing the end of the drama; and I should really feel sorry if anything happened to Bug-Jargal, for he was really a famous fellow."

Paschal removed from his lips the mouth of his wicker-covered flask, and said—

"I would give twelve dozen of port to have seen the cocoa-nut cup that he emptied at a draught."

Alfred, who was gently humming the air of a love-song, interrupted himself by asking Henri to tie his aguilettes; then he added—

"The negro interests me very much, but I have not dared to ask D'Auverney if he knew the air of 'Beautiful Padilla.'"

"What a villain that Biassou was," continued Paschal; "but for all that he knew the value of a Frenchman's word; but there are people more pitiless than Biassou—my creditors, for instance."

"But what do you think of D'Auverney's story?" asked Henri.

"Ma foi," answered Alfred, "I have not paid much attention to it; but I certainly had expected something more interesting from D'Auverney's lips, and then I want to know the air to which Bug-Jargal sang his songs. In fact, I must admit that the story has bored me a little."

"You are right," returned Paschal, the aide-de-camp. "Had I not had my pipe and my bottle, I should have passed but a dreary evening. Besides, there were a lot of absurdities in it; how can we believe, for instance, that that little thief of a sorcerer—I forget his name—would have drowned himself for the sake of destroying his enemy?"

Henri interrupted him with a smile.

"You cannot understand any one taking to water, can you, Captain Paschal? But what struck me more than anything was, that every time D'Auverney mentioned the name of Bug-Jargal his lame dog lifted up his head."

The sound of the sentry carrying arms warned them of D'Auverney's return. All remained silent. He walked up and down the tent for a few moments with folded arms, without a word.

Old Sergeant Thaddeus, who had returned with him, bent over Rask, and furtively caressed him, hoping by that means to conceal his countenance, which was full of anxiety, from the eyes of his captain. At length, after making a strong effort, D'Auverney continued his narrative.

CHAPTER LV.

Rask followed us. The highest rock in the valley was not yet lighted by the rays of the sun; a glimmer of light touched it for an instant, and then passed away.

The negro trembled, and grasped my hand firmly.

"Listen," said he.

A dull sound like the discharge of a piece of artillery was heard, and was repeated by the echoes of the valleys.

"It is the signal," said the negro in a gloomy voice. "It was a cannon shot, was it not?"

I nodded in sign of the affirmative.

In two bounds he sprang to the top of a lofty rock; I followed him. He crossed his arms and smiled sadly.

"Do you see that?" asked he.

I looked in the direction to which he pointed, and on the lofty peak to which he had drawn my attention during our last interview with Marie, and which was now glowing in the rays of the setting sun, I saw a huge black flag, its folds flapping idly in the breeze.

(At this point of his recital D'Auverney again paused.)

I learned afterwards that Biassou, in a hurry to leave his ground, had ordered the flag to be hoisted without waiting for the return of the negroes who had been despatched to assist at my execution. Bug-Jargal was still in the same position—his arms folded, and his eyes eagerly fixed upon the fatal signal.

Suddenly he started, and seemed about to descend from his post of observation.

"Great heavens! my unfortunate comrades!" cried he. "Did you hear the gun?"

I made no reply.

"It was the signal, my brother. They are leading them now to the place of execution."

His head fell upon his breast; after a short pause, he said—

"Go, brother, and rejoice your wife; Rask will guide you to her;" and he whistled an African air, which Rask appeared to recognize, for he wagged his tail, and seemed ready to set out.

Bug-Jargal grasped my hand, and strove to smile, but his features were contracted, and his look was ghastly.

"Farewell for ever!" cried he, and dashed into the thicket by which we were surrounded.

I remained motionless; the little that I understood of the position made me fear the worst.

Rask, on seeing his master disappear, advanced to the edge of the rock, and, raising his head, uttered a plaintive howl. Then he turned to me, his tail was between his legs and his eyes were moist; he looked at me with an air of inquietude, and turned to the spot from which his master had disappeared, and barked several times. I understood him, and shared his fears. Suddenly he dashed off in pursuit of his master, and I should soon have lost sight of him, had he not every now and then halted to give me time to come up to him. In this manner we passed through many a valley and leafy glade; we climbed hills and crossed streams. At last——

D'Auverney's voice failed him, an expression of despair covered his face, and he could not find words to continue his narrative.

"Continue it, Thaddeus," said he, "for I can go on no further."

The old sergeant was not less distressed than his captain, but he made an effort to obey him.

"With your permission, gentlemen," said he, "and since it is your wish, captain, I must tell you, gentlemen, that Bug-Jargal—otherwise called Pierrot—was a tall negro, very strong, very gentle, and the bravest man in the world—except you, captain, if you please; but I was terribly prejudiced against him, for which I will never pardon myself, though you, captain, have forgiven me; so much so, that, when we heard that your execution had been fixed for the evening of the second day, I flew into a furious rage with the poor fellow, and I felt a fiendish pleasure in informing him that his death would pay for yours, or that, if he escaped, ten of his men would be shot by way of reprisal. He said nothing upon hearing this, but an hour afterwards he made his escape through a great hole which he pierced in the wall of his prison."

D'Auverney made a movement of impatience, and Thaddeus continued:

"Well, when we saw the great black flag hoisted on the mountain—and as the negro had not returned, a fact which surprised none of us—our officers ordered the signal gun to be fired, and I was ordered to conduct the ten negroes to the place of execution, a spot we call the Devil's Mouth, about—but it does not matter how far it was from the camp. Well, as you can imagine, we did not take them there to set them at liberty, but I had them bound, as is the custom, and paraded my firing party, when who should burst upon us but the tall negro. He was out of breath with the speed that he had made.

"Good evening, Thaddeus,' said he. 'I am in time.'

"No, gentlemen, he did not utter another word, but hastened to unbind his comrades. I stood there in stupefaction. Then—with your permission, captain—there was a good deal of generous argument between the other negroes and himself, which might have lasted longer but—well, it is no good hiding the fact, it was I that stopped it. At any rate, he took their place. Then the great dog came, poor Rask; he leapt at my throat: he ought to have held me longer, but Pierrot made a sign to him, and the poor brute released me, but his master could not prevent his taking his place at my feet. Then, believing that you were dead, captain—well, I was in a fine rage; I gave the word, Bug-Jargal fell, and a bullet broke the dog's foot.

"Since that time, gentlemen," continued the sergeant, sadly, "he has been lame. Then I heard groans in the adjacent wood; I reached it, and found you—a stray bullet had hit you as you were running forward to save the tall negro. Yes, captain, you were wounded, but Bug-Jargal was dead!

"We carried you back to the camp; you were not dangerously wounded, and the doctors soon cured you, but I believe Madame Marie's nursing had a good deal to do with it."

The sergeant stopped in his story, and D'Auverney, in a solemn voice, added—

"Bug-Jargal was dead!"

Thaddeus bowed his head.

"Yes," said he, "he spared my life, and I—I killed him."

EPILOGUE.

The reader, in general, is seldom satisfied with the conclusion of a narrative unless it enters into every detail in winding up the story. For this reason the minutest researches have been made into the facts having reference to the concluding details of the last scenes of Leopold d'Auverney's life, as well as those of his sergeant and the dog Rask.

The reader is already aware that the captain's feelings of melancholy arose partly from the death of Bug-Jargal, otherwise called Pierrot; but they are not acquainted with the fact that those feelings were terribly increased by the loss of his beloved Marie, who, after having been preserved from the horrors that attended the taking of Fort Galifet, perished in the burning of Cap which took place some weeks later.

The fate of Leopold d'Auverney may be briefly recapitulated. A great victory had been won by the Republican forces against one of those united European armies which so often struggled vainly against our soldiers; and the General of Division, who was in command of the entire force, was seated in his tent drawing up, from the reports of his staff, the bulletin which was to be sent to the National Convention concerning the victory of the day before. As he was thus occupied, an aide-de-camp announced to him the arrival of a Representative of the People, who demanded an audience. The general loathed these ambassadors of the guillotine, who were sent by the party of the Mountain to humiliate the military officers, and too often to demand the heads of the most gallant of the men who had fought bravely for the Republic; looking upon them as chartered informers charged with the hateful mission of spying upon glory. But it would have been dangerous for him to have refused to admit him, especially after such a victory as had resulted to the arms of the Republic.

The gory idol which France had then set up almost invariably demanded victims of the highest lineage, and the executioners of the Place de la Revolution were delighted if they could at the same time cause a head and a coronet to fall—were it one of thorns, like that of Louis XVI.; of flowers, like those of the girls of Verdun; or of laurels like those of Custine or of André Chénier. The general, therefore, gave immediate orders that the Representative of the People should be introduced to his presence.

After a few clumsy congratulations regarding the recent victory, the Representative of the People came up close to the general, and muttered in a suppressed voice—

"But this is not all, Citizen General; it is not enough to destroy the foreign enemy—those nearer home must be also crushed."

"What do you mean, Citizen Representative?" asked the astonished general.

"There is in your division," answered the emissary of the Convention, in an unpleasant manner, "a captain named Leopold d'Auverney, who is serving in the 32nd Brigade; do you know him, general?"

"Know him, certainly I do," replied the general; "only as you came in I was reading the report of the Adjutant General which refers to him. The 32nd Brigade had in him an excellent officer, and I was about to recommend him for promotion."

"What, Citizen General?" interposed the representative, harshly, "were you thinking of promoting him?"

"Such was most certainly my intention, citizen."

"Victory has blinded you, general," cried the representative, imperiously; "take care what you say or do. If you cherish serpents who are the enemies of the people, take care that the people do not crush you and the serpents at the same moment. This Leopold d'Auverney is an aristocrat, a hater of the revolution, a royalist, a Girondin! Public justice demands his head, and he must be given up to me on the spot."

"I cannot do so," replied the general, coldly.

"*How! you cannot do so?*" shouted the representative, whose rage was redoubled at this opposition. "Are you ignorant, general, of the extent of my power? I, in the name of the Republic, command you, and you have no option but to obey. Listen to me: in consideration of your recent success, I will read you the report which has been handed in regarding this D'Auverney, and which I shall send with him to the Public Prosecutor. 'Leopold Auverney (formerly known as D'Auverney), captain in the 32nd Brigade, is convicted of having, at a meeting of conspirators, narrated an anti-revolutionary tale, conducing to the ridicule of the true principles of Equality and Liberty, and exalting the worn-out superstitions known under the names of *royalty* and *religion*. Convicted, secondly, of having used expressions deservedly forbidden by all good republicans, to describe certain recent events, notably those referring to the negroes of Saint Domingo. Convicted thirdly, of having made use of the expression *Monsieur* instead of *Citizen* during the whole of his narrative; and, by the said narrative, of having endeavoured to bring into contempt the Republic one and indivisible, and also to propagate the infamous doctrines of the Girondins.' Death is the punishment for these crimes, and I demand his body. Do you hesitate, general, to hand this traitor over to me, to meet the well-merited punishment of his crimes?"

"Citizen," answered the general, with dignity, "this enemy of his country has given his life for her. As a contrast to your report, listen to an extract from mine. 'Leopold d'Auverney, captain in the 32nd Brigade, has contributed largely to the success that our arms have obtained. A formidable earthwork had been erected by the allies; it was the key to their position, and it was absolutely necessary to carry it at the point of the bayonet. It was an almost impregnable position, and the death of the stormers who led the attack was almost inevitable. Captain d'Auverney volunteered to lead the forlorn hope; he carried the earthwork, but was shot down at the moment of victory. Sergeant Thaddeus of the 32nd, and a large dog, were found dead within a few paces of him.' It was my intention to propose that the National Convention should pass a vote that the Captain Leopold d'Auverney had merited the thanks of his country. You see, Citizen Representative," continued the general, calmly, "that our duties differ slightly—we both send a report to the Convention. The same name appears in each list: you denounce him as a traitor, I hold him up to posterity as a hero. You devote him to ignominy, I to glory; you would erect a scaffold for him, whilst I propose a statue in his honour. He is fortunate in having, by death in action, escaped the infamy you proposed for him. He whose death you desired is dead—he has not waited for you."

Furious at seeing his conspiracy disappear with the conspirator, the Representative muttered—

"Dead, is he?—more's the pity."

The general caught his words, and in indignant tones exclaimed—

"There is still something left for you, Citizen Representative. Go seek for the body of Captain d'Auverney amongst the ruins of the redoubt. Who can tell if the bullets of the enemy may not have spared his head for his country's guillotine?"

www.ingramcontent.com/pod-product-compliance
Lightning Source LLC
Chambersburg PA
CBHW030110170426
43198CB00009B/560